Why Bother Looking?

Finding God in Your Seasons of Life

_____

By
Lynn Jarrett

authorHOUSE™

1663 LIBERTY DRIVE, SUITE 200
BLOOMINGTON, INDIANA 47403
(800) 839-8640
WWW.AUTHORHOUSE.COM

First published by AuthorHouse 08/03/05

ISBN: 1-4208-5451-8 (sc)

Printed in the United States of America
Bloomington, Indiana

This book is printed on acid-free paper.

ENDORSEMENTS

Our perception of God can be easily blurred by our own life experiences. Lynn Jarrett identifies the seasons of our life that impede our clear focus of God's true nature. Her professional observations, self-disclosing journey, and excellent self-assessing tools offer every reader the opportunity to gain personal insight of self in viewing God. The revealing heart-felt truths provide a framework to discover and experience God that gives freedom, hope and purpose for every season of life!

Dr. Nicholas Phillips D.Min. LLMFT
Pastor, FamilyLife ministries educator, & therapist

Trying to put the pieces together? Disoriented? If so, "Why Bother Looking?" is masterfully crafted to show your seasons of life and helps you find your authentic path. It's a perfect gift...in more ways than one.

Lisa Mininni
President, Excellerate Associates
Founder, The C Club for Cancer Conquerers

Lynn Jarrett in her book "Why Bother Looking" causes one to reflect on your own seasons of life. With her vulnerable and honest personal sharing of her life journey, she enables the reader to personally connect to the person behind the words on the written page. This book offers amazing hope from the pain of the past and springs you into new opportunities for the future with purpose, a mission and a joy that can only be found in faith.

Lillian M. Easterly
Care Ministries Pastor
NorthRidge Church

I not only received your book today but also, read your book today. Well done! I had no intention of reading it cover to cover but you hooked me with the first chapter. Excellent and easy read. May this be the first of many!

J.C. Brown
Retired executive

To my mom, who can now enjoy her spring and summer seasons in Heaven.

To my beloved husband, whose unconditional love carries me through all our seasons of life.

WHY BOTHER LOOKING?

ACKNOWLEDGEMENTS

With heartfelt thanks:

To all my NSA and coaching colleagues who encouraged me to write this book in the first place, thank you for pushing me forward when I needed it!

To my peer reviewers who took the time and effort to give honest feedback and thoughtful suggestions. Thank you, Lisa, John, Mary, Jess, Christine, and Jon.

To the current and former clients, and friends who serve as a common thread for the theme of this book, I thank you for allowing me to share your stories as an inspiration to others in their seasons of life.

To Pat, my editor, I thank you for your wonderful wisdom, feedback, and suggestions. Your partnership on this book made it even more fun to write.

To my precious daughters, thank you for your patience and understanding while I wrote this book. My hope is that this book and your faith will serve as an inspiration to others in their seasons of life.

To my deceased mother, although she chose to live her life in the coldest winter season, it served as an inspiration to me to help others see that there are three other life seasons worth living.

To my husband, Jon, your support, encouragement, love and commitment over the years have helped me become the woman God designed me to be. Thank you for being my best friend, confidante and teammate.

I thank God for equipping me, saving me, and loving me. I have been privileged to work with so many wonderful people over the years and could not have done it without His wisdom, strength and faithfulness.

INTRODUCTION

When I began my work as a therapist, my goal was to help people heal so that they could lead full, productive lives. As a Christian, I was able to integrate Biblical principles with different schools of psychology, which allowed for a more eclectic approach to my work. Client after client would come to me with a similar story: "I want and need more out of my counseling. There has got to be more to counseling than just talking about feelings and taking a rational approach to changing thoughts and behaviors!" These clients sought out a Christian counselor because they wanted a more holistic approach. They noticed a need to develop their spiritual side.

When people are in crisis, they are apt to either run completely away from God or run to Him. My clients were tired of having to depend on themselves to fix their lives. They wanted something more and they sought out God. If my clients were comfortable with the idea, I would open and close our sessions in prayer. The prayers would provide comfort, courage and strength to move forward with tough issues they never thought they could handle. The more strength they received from God to conquer the issues that brought them to counseling in the first place, the more willing they were to seek out a church to help them grow spiritually.

When I switched careers to be a life and business coach, I noticed a similar pattern. These successful, motivated and well-educated clients felt something was missing from their lives. Even after achieving their success, they wanted more. The more they had, the more they wanted. But what they had didn't seem to fill that void. They were tired of running the rat race and wanted a new direction. "Is this as good as it gets?" they asked. Although I was hired to be their business coach, every client had personal needs that were eventually addressed in the coaching sessions. Often our coaching would approach one's spiritual side, or lack thereof. Many discovered that approaching life and work with some spiritual basis that included God allowed for better clarity of direction, evaluation of priorities, and overall improvement personally and professionally. They were content, experienced greater satisfaction, and approached their lives and careers with a more positive outlook.

Over the years, I have encountered people who want to spit nails if the word God is even mentioned. It is obvious they are angry with God, yet they have absolutely no interest in talking about why. Experience has shown me that many people perpetuate their anger towards God by *not* ever talking about or addressing the issue. Why? Many believe it to be true that if they stay angry and ignore the issue completely, it won't have any impact on their lives. They can go about living their lives and feel no repercussions from their anger and neglect. Completely ignoring one's spiritual side is like trying to hold a balloon under water; it keeps popping up. Can you say that your work is completely separate from your personal life? If you are divorced, can you say you were never married? Can you say your kids are not part of your family? The answer is no to these questions because you cannot separate something that is essentially a part of you. Everyone has a spiritual side. Whether you acknowledge it or not is your choice.

I asked a friend of mine to read this book. He answered with an emphatic "no!" My friend said he didn't feel the book applied to him because he isn't angry with God; it was organized religion that he didn't like. He'd had some negative experiences with church as a child. Chapter two discusses this very issue of how past religious experiences impact your view of God. I challenged him and said that if that were the case, then there was no harm in reading about God since that wasn't the source of his anger. He declined. He chose not to look at the reasons behind his resistance to the topic of God, which is why I wrote this book.

This book is designed for anyone who has anger or bitterness towards God or organized religion. Reading this book can help you quit trying to keep the balloon under water! You may be wondering, "What could this book possibly say that I don't already know? I am not interested in finding out about a God who doesn't care about me and whom I care nothing about as well." If that is the case, I invite you to journey with me through this book to investigate once and for all if God could be real in your life.

This book applies to you if you:
1. are just curious about God's role in you life.
2. have been disillusioned or disappointed by your religious upbringing.
3. once had God as a part of your life, but no longer.
4. have had life experiences that made you bitter or angry towards God.

While the stories in this book are true, identifying characteristics of the clients discussed have been changed to protect their confidentiality and identity. The stories of my own struggles are my gift to you. The hand that has guided me is also guiding you. The love that sustains me is available for you as well.

PART I

INVESTIGATING THIS "GOD" THING

CHAPTER 1

YOUR ROAD OF LIFE

"Really, I'm not searching!" These were the words of a client who was adamant about not bringing God into his counseling process. He was fed up with religious people who said they loved God, yet seemed to judge everyone and everything. "If these people represent God, then I want no part of it!" he said.

"Well, that's quite an assumption to make about all religious people. Has something recently happened to spur this anger?"

For the next thirty minutes, he spoke through clenched teeth and a raised voice, recounting a recent experience at a church he had visited with his girlfriend, who had just broken up with him. His eyes conveyed disgust, sadness, frustration, and confusion.

"What happened at this church that made you so angry?" I asked.

"The pastor was talking about the need to turn to God in the good times and the bad and that He knows what's best for us. I totally disagree! I know what's best for me, and I don't need God to direct my life and keep me from what I want to do!"

"And you think that if God is part of your life, somehow you'd lose your freedom?"

"Absolutely! I have done just fine without God all these years. He never was there before, and I pride myself in the fact that I have done everything on my own. I'm successful today because I made it happen, not God!"

Mirroring his resistance (a counseling technique) and reflecting his need for self-sufficiency, I said "Sounds like you're pretty self-sufficient and you don't need anyone else. You have it all figured out. No wonder your girlfriend left you."

Silence. He glared at me, and then shifted his eyes and body. I hit a nerve.

"What brought you here today?" I asked.

"I don't know," he said in a small, shaky voice.

"I seem to have hit a nerve with you and I can understand you don't want to talk about it right now. Is there anything you'd like to say before we close out this session?" He was silent. "Here's my card. If you think you'd like to come back at another time to discuss it, my door is always open." He grabbed my card and stomped out of my office.

One month later, he came back. He stayed in counseling for more than a year. As the weeks and months unfolded, this man was willing to take a look at how his self-sufficiency was a positive and a negative force in his life. He learned how to take care of himself at a very young age because his parents were physically and emotionally absent many times throughout his childhood and teen years. He paid his own way through college. He was able to land a good job with a company that would allow him to move up the corporate ladder. He had a lot of career success, but he was very lonely. He had no one with whom to share his success. For two months he blamed God for not putting a wife and family in his life. His greatest need was to connect with other people on a more personal level. When he discovered he was responsible for his lack of personal relationships, his view of God shifted. He learned to look to God for guidance rather than as the scapegoat. We prayed at the beginning and the end of our sessions. He started sharing more feelings in the counseling sessions, and began to trust that I would be physically and emotionally present – something he never allowed himself to experience because of the precedent his parents set.

By the time this client finished counseling, he was able to take responsibility for his contribution to his unhappy life and what caused him to get there. His contributions included mistrust of others, workaholism, arrogance, belittling people if they couldn't do the work his way (he was a manager), unrealistic expectations of people at work and in personal life, and being a perfectionist.

The counseling process helped him let go of his perfectionism and his need to work eighty plus hours a week. This allowed him some free time to devote to building relationships. He realized that the way he built his career and got results were very different from how he approaches personal relationships. He opened up his heart and mind to allow God to help him see life differently. He started attending a church that had many different small groups he could join and get to know people at a more intimate level. He saw that those people were not 'fake' as he had perceived religious people to be. Once he allowed himself to experience God rather than make assumptions, he learned he could *live* life rather than just *do* life.

WHERE IN THE FOREST ARE YOU?

Imagine you are in a forest. In your current life, where would you place yourself in the forest?

A. In the thicket where you see only trees
B. In a clearing in your thicket
C. Out of the forest and on the road to your destination?

IN THE THICKET

A newlywed couple was enjoying their first year of marriage. She trusted him with the finances and assumed he was taking care of the bills. One day when she was cleaning around the house, she saw a stack of unpaid bills, final notices, and statements on his student loans that she thought had been paid off. Along with these notices, she also noticed a stack of receipts for items he bought to spruce up his car. She never realized he spent that much money on his car. When she confronted him on the poor money management, he just brushed it off and said there was plenty of money.

Do you ever have days, weeks, months or years where you can't seem to see beyond the thicket of your situation(s)? No matter which way you turn to try to gain direction, you find yourself going in circles? The more you try to resolve a situation, the more you find yourself beyond knee-deep and becoming waist-deep in the thicket. You ask yourself, "How did I get here? How do I get out of this?" Frustration, confusion and a sense of hopelessness often accompany a person in this scenario. Maybe your thicket is a bad marriage or relationship, a job you absolutely hate, lingering bitterness towards a person or situation, or financial stress. Perhaps you believe any or all attempts have been made to try to get yourself out of the thicket, but nothing seems to work. You have taken others' advice, come up with your own ideas, or ignored the situation and hoped it would just go away. But nothing has worked. What is a person to do?

Sometimes in a thicket, you encounter a snake and get bit. A snakebite can be a surprise that seems to compound your problem. What was the snakebite for this couple? It took the husband losing his job to finally get a wake up call that they were financially in trouble. His company was downsizing and the husband was unprepared. He assumed he'd retire at this company. It took him eight months to find another job in his profession.

What were some of the lessons they were forced to learn during their difficult financial crisis?

1. Talked to a credit counselor and attended money management classes at their church and learned how to reduce their debt...slowly.

2. Had to take a serious look at their lifestyle and where the money was going. The money management classes showed them how to budget, and they realized that the husband's car habit was costing them an average of $2,000 a month. That money was quickly dispersed to pay off credit cards and bills past due.

3. They learned to live lean during those months before he got another job. When they saw how little they really needed to survive, they gained a new perspective on money, and were even more committed to paying off their debt quickly.

Sometimes it takes a snakebite to get you to jump out of your thicket and into a clearing so you can really see and understand your circumstances.

Suggestions for avoiding snakebites in your life:

1. *Never assume.*   The husband in the above scenario assumed job security. Being surprised when that assumption is blown away throws you into a 'crisis mode' that can give you the sense of helplessness or hopelessness. This can lead to feelings of being 'trapped' in your situation and seeing no way out. What assumptions are you currently making about the people and situations in your life?

2. *Be prepared.* This does not mean to live life as if you are waiting for 'the other shoe to drop,' but rather it means developing a preventative way of preparing for the "what if's" in life. Let's go back to the above couple's scenario. Had they saved more than they spent, they might have felt less stress and pressure before the husband landed another job. What about the case of divorce, when one partner might be totally unprepared? If all other avenues to salvage the marriage (counseling, mediation, etc) fail, then surrounding yourself with support systems of people, divorce recovery groups and legal resources can help you prepare for the lifestyle change.

3. *Evaluate yourself.*   The client I described in the beginning chose to take a step back and evaluate the negative contributions and decisions he made in his life. Ask yourself the following questions:

     A. What is my 'thicket' situation?

    B. How did I get here? (Make a 'roadmap' of decisions you believe have lead up to your current thicket.)

    C. Was it based on some poor decisions I made? Did I misjudge people or myself?

4. *Trust in something other than self or others.* I am amazed over the years how many people say they don't care about God, yet when their thicket situation appears, they wind up praying. When a situation doesn't turn out the way a person wants it to, he or she goes back to blaming God. God always gives us what we need, not always what we want. When I think back to times I was upset with God about how a situation ended, I was able to see that it turned out better than what I actually wanted.

SEE A CLEARING

A young man was devastated when his two-year marriage ended. The first four times he came into my office, he wept through his entire counseling sessions. He was in complete shock and was grieving over the tremendous loss. Even though he came from a religious upbringing, he felt numb towards God and didn't feel he knew how or what to pray for. He was in the coldest, darkest season of his life. He was devastated because the day before his wife told him she wanted a divorce, she cleaned out their savings account to run off with another man. He found out about the money a week later when he tried taking some out to pay for an attorney. She also had set up a separate account where she was transferring some of their checking account to her personal account. She handled their financial matters because she was an accountant by profession. He had trusted her with their finances and assumed everything was okay because they made a comfortable living. During this tough time, his friends really stepped in and found an excellent attorney who helped him fight back so that he would regain some of his money and be left with more than just his dignity in the end.

He had found his clearing through the thicket by continuing his counseling, being involved in a divorce recovery group and receiving support from family and friends. His counseling allowed him to do a lot of soul searching during his time in the thicket, but he saw a clearing and learned some skills for getting back on the road to living. Some of the skills he learned to get to his clearing were:

1. *Setting boundaries.* I had him read two books on how to set boundaries*, recognize safe people** and become a safe person himself.

2. *Being prepared.* If he were to marry again, requiring they both agree to premarital counseling to prepare for a lifelong marriage. He wanted to know everything beforehand because he realized he and his ex-wife rushed into marriage. He wanted a marriage that was going to last.

3. *Having a spiritual foundation.* He started attending church regularly to regain the spiritual side he let go for many years. He saw that leaving God out of his life lead him down a road to his wife, who was an untrustworthy person.

4. *Defining goals.* He learned to define more personal and professional goals, which he had not done for the two years he was married.

5. *Trusting God first.* He gained patience in understanding that it would take time for him to trust again. He realized that his starting

---

* *"Boundaries" by Henry Cloud & John Townsend.*
** *"Safe People" by Henry Cloud & John Townsend.*

point in trusting others was learning how to trust God again.

Perhaps you have been through some of life's "rough waters" and are now able to see some "light at the end of the tunnel." The hopelessness and confusion turn to a hope that you are now on the right track. Others may find the clearing uncomfortable and cannot stay in the clearing because they are waiting for the "other shoe to drop" to dash their hopes that they are truly out of the thicket. Wherever you place yourself, and depending on how long you were in the thicket, you either run to the clearing or walk gingerly towards it. You are happy to have gotten to this place, but may not have the life skills or tools to get you on the road where you truly want to go. What's keeping you from reaching the road? Ask yourself these questions:

1. Do I see what's on the road and am I afraid of it?
2. Do I believe I might have to make changes for which I believe am not yet ready?
3. I see the road represents something I cannot control. Am I afraid to give up control?
4. Do I truly believe I'd be happier staying in my thicket?
5. Is the clearing my comfort zone that I don't want to change?

If you answered "yes" to any of the above questions, read on to see what lies on the road for you.

ON THE ROAD

Now that you feel you are a strong person for having come through tough circumstances and worked yourself onto the road and feel there is no turning back, do you truly know where you're heading? There are plenty of us who overcome circumstances only to find ourselves in the thicket again with another person or situation. You ask yourself, "How did I get here this time?" This is called living in crisis mode. You thrive on living from crisis to crisis because this is your modus operandi.

A person is walking on a sidewalk on a busy street but doesn't notice a large hole in the sidewalk. This person falls in. The second time this person sees the hole, but still falls in. The third time, this person tries to walk around the hole, but still falls in. The fourth time this person walks down the street, he walks on the other side of the street and a different sidewalk. This person had to fall in the same hole three separate times in order to learn that the hole is not going away. How you approach the hole makes the difference. Do you do the same thing over and over again expecting different results? This is the definition of insanity. Or do you do different things and get different results? Whatever you find yourself doing, it comes down to a matter of choice. You can choose to acknowledge mistakes and use them to learn and grow, or you can get caught up in blaming people and circumstances for putting you in the thicket and plow forward on your road without having any idea if you're heading in the right direction. Do you see where your road is leading you?

A business colleague had a bout with cancer at the young age of 26. She was climbing up the corporate ladder quickly and often worked seventy plus hours weekly. She was ambitious, driven and successful at what she did. She had noticed the swollen lymph nodes behind her ears but ignored them for months because she was always too busy to go in to the doctor. One day while sitting in a meeting, she noticed her right lymph node was particularly large. Alarmed, she went to the doctor the following week. The doctor was shocked by the size and did an immediate biopsy, which indeed confirmed cancer. When she first got her diagnosis, she tried bargaining with God: "Okay, if I say all my prayers and do good, will you let me come out of this alive?"

Her snakebite was the cancer diagnosis. Her thicket came in the form of her chemo and radiation therapy. Her clearing was evaluating her life and what mattered most. She saw the need to include God to provide the strength to help her through her chemo and realized that even though she felt she could control her career success, she couldn't completely control the outcome of the chemo. Fortunately, they caught it early enough and with aggressive chemo and radiation, she has been in remission for over 13 years. When she was receiving therapy, she was definitely in the thicket. When she received the results that her therapy rid her of the cancer, she was able to see a clearing, but realized that cancer had changed the way she thought and lived. Her road of life now looked different. A life coach helped her regain her confidence to explore who she had become.

I believe God gives us our thickets, clearings, and roads to evaluate our lives and where we are heading. What are you willing to learn through your different situations? What is guiding your steps?

WHAT DO YOU USE FOR YOUR COMPASS?

How do you know you're on the right road? What resources do you use to know and feel comfortable with where you are heading? Do you rely on people or circumstances to guide your business deals, personal relationships, or financial decisions? What happens when your resources fail you? Often you toughen up, move on, and learn to trust little. You become your own resource and educate yourself to be well informed so you don't have to rely on others or circumstances. You pride yourself on how well you do, yet yearn for life not to be so burdensome. Somehow it never seems enough. There is always something more or better you believe you must do to stay 'on top of your game.' You are proud of your success, but at what cost? Do you find yourself emotionally and physically exhausted? Are you passionate about the life you are leading?

When life gets overwhelming, a person can turn to negative forms of coping with the stresses of life. These become 'broken compasses'. You may not realize you are following a broken compass until you look at it and tap it. Then you realize you have been following the wrong direction. You can continue on the wrong road for a long time.

A 'broken compass' can look like:
1. an addiction (work, alcohol or other drugs, gambling, promiscuity, unhealthy relationships, etc.) that becomes an escape
2. a mentor's advice that is always followed without question
3. a successful career without any life balance
4. self-esteem that is reliant on material possessions (cars, large house, social clubs, boat, etc.)
5. self-esteem that is reliant on how well you perform in your career.

WHAT'S YOUR FRAMEWORK?

My five year-old daughter and I just cracked open a new 100-piece puzzle. She loves to do puzzles, but needed help in putting it together. As we were starting the puzzle, my advice to her was to piece the frame of the puzzle first, then fill in the rest.

It dawned on me how often we try to live life without a framework from which to work and play. There have been plenty of times in building my business that without a constant evaluation of my business plan, I'd skip to what I thought was a great opportunity, and then would be upset when it didn't pan out. In the early months of working as a solo entrepreneur, I constantly changed my niche. At first I thought I was going to work strictly with small business owners, then with individuals who only wanted life coaching, then with corporate sales people, and on and on. I went where the wind blew. Whatever my circumstances were or whoever was my latest coaching client that was my focus. I tried piecing together a puzzle, but I had no idea what the picture looked like. It wasn't until I took advantage of some small business resources, received more professional business coach training, and found a business partner to develop a business plan that the business started taking shape and forming a beautiful puzzle. I now have a puzzle picture as my reference. Unless I keep in mind my original plan, I lose track of my framework.

SKIING ANYONE?

The last time my husband and I went downhill skiing (notice how I said last time?!), our chairlift took us to an advanced hill that neither my husband nor I were experienced enough to ski down. I was scared of this very steep run. My husband said, "If you fall down, just get back up." He had forgotten how just an hour earlier I had a big fall and had great difficulty getting back up. From the top of the hill, the bottom looked far away and the trip downhill seemed insurmountable. There were icy patches everywhere on the hill. I decided the only way I was to get down the hill alive was to snow plow my way down. Sure I looked funny, but I didn't care. A woman came screaming down as she passed me, saying, "I'll never make it!" As she whizzed by, I yelled to her, "Don't look down; just look at what's in front of you!"

How about you? Do you believe that life looks insurmountable, that there is no way you'll get down your hill safely? Can you stick with what is right in front of you instead of focusing on the icy patches and the bottom of the hill? Do you ever look at situations or decisions that seem insurmountable, yet ignore the ice patches or trouble spots along the way even though those spots are trying to say "Slow down!"

Once I arrived down at the end of the run safely, I looked back up at the top and thought "Thank you, God!" How often can we trust that our own strength and confidence will make it through a tough spot? If we are to really look back at a situation, there was something else helping us down the hill safely. Thinking back on a tough situation that zapped your physical and emotional energy, what brought you through that? Can you say it was completely your own doing?

ONLY ONE TRUE NORTH

Anyone who has ever camped with a compass knows that there is only one true north. No matter how lost you are, the night sky (as long as it's not cloudy) will always show the North Star, which is the brightest. It is constant, unchanging, and reliable and can never be disputed. Can you say the same for the resources you have relied on for your entire life? No. It is not humanly possible. There will always be someone who will disappoint you. There will always be something that will disappoint you that will make you question its validity and reliability.

For example, a wife always relied on her husband to financially provide for the family, but he wound up gambling away their savings. She was devastated to find out the man she thought she could trust cannot be trusted. Her reliance was on another human being.

Another example would be someone placing all his esteem and confidence into his career, and when he loses his job due to downsizing, he doesn't know where to turn. The promotions, the work, and the money gave him worth, and now it doesn't matter how great of a worker he was. His reliance was on an assumption that his work would always bring him value.

Whether your North Star has been a person or a thing, you use your life experience as your 'lab' to confirm or deny your hypotheses.

YOUR HYPOTHESIS OF GOD

So, if you have used your life experiences to test God, how did He do? Has he failed miserably? Have you found Him to be invalid and unreliable? Have you noticed God at times, yet find Him inconsistent? These are probably characteristics you would use to describe your human experience with people and circumstances and have transferred that to God. Fair enough. But I would like to offer the possibility that there is a factor to consider investigating: your perception of God must transcend your human mindset to see God for who He really is—a supernatural being. We impose human characteristics on a supernatural being. No wonder we don't understand God, especially if we have never taken the time to get to know Him! I invite you to discover what your life really means with and without God. In order to do this, you must start with where your perception of God began and how life has evolved around this perception.

CHAPTER 2

YOUR PERCEPTION OF GOD

I grew up in a dysfunctional home; I was the youngest of four children. By the time I was seven, my life experiences included: an alcoholic mother, rageaholic father, all forms of abuse, foster homes, and then (to our relief) my parent's divorce when I was seven.

When I was four years old, I remember my mom dressing up my middle sister and me for church on a snowy Saturday. We never made it to church because my mom passed out drunk behind the wheel and crashed the car into a tree a few blocks from our house. My sister and I were okay, but my mom had to be taken to the hospital for cuts and bruises. Two weeks after the car crash, my siblings and I were put in foster homes.

On a snowy night in December, the Department of Children and Family Services delivered us to our first foster home where all four of us children stayed until we could be placed in separate homes. I remember being whisked away from home and hearing my siblings screaming and crying not to be taken away from Mom and Dad. Four days after arriving at our first foster home, I spent my fifth birthday with complete strangers. The wish I made with the candles I blew out was to go back home. It would be six months before we were able to return home. During those six months, my mom was court-ordered to alcohol rehab, and my dad was court-ordered to the psychiatric hospital for the two domestic abuse charges against him.

I was always terrified of my dad. His yelling and the times the police were sent to our home to intervene and keep my dad from beating up on mom always kept me in my room with a pillow over my ears to try and drown out the chaos. I stayed far away from the fighting because when my dad was done yelling at mom, he'd start on my older siblings. When I was six, I accidentally hit my friend with a ball in the back of her head and caused her nose to hit a metal fire engine truck. She started crying and ran to tell my dad what I did. My dad took her side and wouldn't even listen to me explain it was an accident. He yelled at me to get inside and that he would deal with me there. I ran into the house crying hysterically because I thought he was going to really hurt me. My mom came into my room and asked what was wrong. I told her "Dad is going to kill me!" She noticed I was so scared and shaky that I wet my pants. My mom told him not to touch me or she would call the police. He apologized later that day for scaring me, but I never let him come near me even when he wasn't mad. I never believed him when he said he loved me. I couldn't trust that he wouldn't hurt me.

My parents divorced when I was seven years old. It was a relief to have quiet in our house. My dad had

Sunday visits with us, so our time was very limited with him. After the divorce I began to believe that no adult could be trusted. My first authority figures in my life taught me not to trust.

To add insult to injury, I attended a parochial school where the rules I followed dictated whether I was a good or bad girl to God. As long as I said my morning prayer along with the pledge of allegiance, went to liturgy practice, never spoke in class unless spoken to and did my weekly duty of Sunday church, then I was okay with God. I needed to do the church sacraments as well so that it would show up on my report card that I was a good girl. I never questioned what would happen to me if I didn't do the things I was told. I figured being quiet and obedient would keep God from punishing me. It worked at home, so I figured it would work with God. I was scared to death of God's punishment if I didn't do what I was supposed to do.

As a result of this childhood environment, I had a very negative view of God. God was absent, angry, distant, inconsistent, mean, unloving, and cruel to me. Yet my religious upbringing told me I had to "practice" God in my life, at the very least, on a weekly basis.

My mother became sober for the first time when I was five years old, but began drinking again when I was eight. My mom's drinking worsened as the years went on, and by the time I reached high school, the physical abuse and drunken stupors were a daily occurrence. I felt helpless and hopeless as if there was no way out of my prison. The only way I saw out of the pain of my prison was to kill myself. For whatever reason, luckily, I never acted on my suicide thoughts. Maybe I had a "fighter" spirit within me and didn't know it. I prided myself on the fact that I was strong and could handle anything. As a result of that strength,

I was seen as a leader at a very early age, and was often told "Wow, you're so mature for your age." Of course I was mature-I was made an adult child from the moment I was born into my chaotic family. I was an adult child, never allowed to be or act like a child as a child. I didn't believe like there was anything or anyone who could protect me except myself.

YOUR PERCEPTION IMPACTS EVERYTHING

Choosing to hold onto your bitter feelings towards God, without attempting to understand and reconcile them, is certainly your decision. But ask yourself this question: If I'm truly content with my (lack of) feelings toward God right now, why did I pick up this book?

My perception of God from my past inventory:
Please put a check next to the statements that are true of your childhood or add your own.

1. I grew up in a very strict home.
2. I was scolded much more than I was praised by my parents.
3. I had (have) feelings of being unworthy and unloved.
4. I pride myself in being successful and ambitious.
5. I had (have) no religious upbringing.
6. My religious upbringing was legalistic (rules, regulations that dictated "good" to God).
7. I was abused as a child (verbally, physically).
8. I have been sexually abused or traumatized.
9. My parents are divorced.
10. One of my parents cheated on the other.
11. I have always rebelled against my religious upbringing.

12. I lived with an addicted parent (alcohol, drugs, work, gambling, sex, etc).
13. I caused problems, which were the only way I could get my parents' attention.
14. My parent(s) was uninvolved in my life.
15. I did not receive emotional support from my parents.
16. I was pampered by my parents.
17. I had a rageaholic parent.
18. I grew up with a single parent.
19. I lived with a hypocritical parent (inconsistent in and outside home).
20. I was diagnosed with a debilitating illness.
21. I was exposed to pornography at a young age.
22. I grew up in an impoverished home.
23. A parent died.
24. My parent relied on me as a companion because of spouse's absence.
25. I had negative interactions with "church" people.
26. Religion was "forced" on me.

If you answered "yes" to any of the above questions, then it might be helpful for you to find ways to work through your negative views rather than around them. As I mentioned before, we sometimes use substitutes for God, such as material possessions, career goals, or addictions, and often times we believe it is easier to just dismiss God (work around it) rather than address (work through it) Him.

You might have noticed that these statements deal with parents. Parents are our first perception of authority figures in our lives. No parents are perfect, and this book is *not* intended to place all the blame for your problems on parents. The inventory is a way of showing just how much your family of origin truly does impact your spiritual decisions.

A friend of mine grew up with a very strict and demanding father. She was often told she wasn't good at anything although she was an excellent student and athlete in high school. Since she never really received approval from her dad, she has spent most of her adult life excelling at her work and working many long hours. She is incredibly performance-driven and is very demanding of herself and others. She does not respect or trust male authority figures and has difficulty hearing God referred to as a "Him." Her earthly father has definitely impacted her view on God. Referring to God as a 'her' does not resonate with her because of her religious upbringing. She had always heard God referred to as a 'him.'

You might also have been negatively impacted by your religious upbringing. For many whose upbringing was unpleasant (including mine), it is as if there is a spoken or unspoken rule that you didn't question the church about its doctrines or sacraments. You just did and believed what you were told. If you tried to explore and discover your own beliefs or had personal experiences with God that were different from what the church taught you, you might have experienced resistance or frustration from your parents. Generations before us didn't question what they were told. If you rebelled against your religious upbringing (as I did), then this would indicate that you are one who doesn't want to be told what to do; you want to find your own way. Often times there is a difference between the religious beliefs you were taught and how you might experience God. God meets us all individually, so our experiences are different.

I had a college friend whose father was a senior minister of a church. When the truth came out that her father had an affair with the church secretary, my friend's world turned upside down. The humiliation, anger, mistrust, and a whole myriad of feelings emerged that knocked my friend off her feet. She rebelled against God and organized religion throughout college and into her first years of marriage. Her rebellion included dating guys she knew her parents wouldn't like; dabbling in witchcraft; drinking heavily for a short time; and blatantly making fun of anyone who mentioned God or religion. Ironically, she and I met through a Christian campus group. My experience has shown me that people who come from a strong religious background (this friend was a pastor's kid) often do rebel but are eventually drawn back to their original religious values. These values take on a different meaning because there is life experience with and without God that has allowed them to *internalize* their faith rather than approach it externally.

In the inventory, if you answered yes to several questions or have admitted that you were abused, it will take some time to work through and bring resolution to this open wound. The pain, hurt, anger and frustration are very real. You have every right to have those emotions. Sprinkled in with the myriad of feelings can be an underlying anger with God. You do have the choice to continue with the bitterness or to become proactive to become better. Denial of the pain will keep you from understanding and experiencing God in a heartfelt way or even giving God a chance. Your approach to God will remain intellectual. You can find counselors who specialize in abuse recovery through professional organizations like the American Psychological Association, or if you do want to include your spiritual side in your healing, the American Association of Christian Counselors. Check with your local mental health agency for support groups or contact a large church in your area for a listing of support groups they offer there. Be proactive and put your past in perspective so you can move on to your future.

LIFE'S CIRCUMSTANCES SHAPE OUR VIEW OF GOD

Have you ever been so frustrated with your life, that you wonder, "Can't I get anything right?" or "I was on such a successful track, and now I can't seem get out of the starting block?" I can relate to that. "Anywhere, but here" is what I tell myself.

I had been a therapist for six years when I decided to change my career path. I loved my work as a counselor, primarily because I was very good at helping others heal from their past, as I had. I enjoyed helping others see the hope and freedom that came from the counseling process.

When I switched careers to become a life and business coach, I imagined the transition would have been a little smoother and I would have maintained the level of income I was used to receiving. I certainly was the idealistic entrepreneur whose reality came crashing down when I realized I really needed to work hard at building my business. When I worked as a therapist, I had a steady stream of referrals, so I never had to go out and build a network to grow my business. What a paradigm shift!

I have found the times I have been bitter toward God have been a result of not being in the *right place, at the right time, for the right reasons*.

NOT THE RIGHT PLACE

My friend thought she had the greatest job. She loved her work as a program manager in an organization that promoted health and wellness for everyone that walked through the doors. She supervised leaders to work effectively with others and learn to take care of themselves as well. Everyone contributed to the vision of the department and where it fit into the organization as a whole.

Everything seemed to be running smoothly until she had a new boss. It was evident within a month that he didn't care about the foundation she and her team had built, but rather had his own agenda for their program. As time went on, he was telling her how to run her people and program, and expected my friend and her team to respect him for it. She found herself jockeying for position, trying to hang on to what was left of the original vision for the program that allowed it to do well. The other leaders noticed how this man was more interested in controlling rather than leading.

She did finally leave that workplace. It wasn't until she was out of the environment that she realized how miserable she was. She saw how the stress affected her eating and sleeping habits, her mood outside of work, and her inability to concentrate at work. She worked with a man who was not at all interested in change or in working more effectively with others. Because she was an innovator by nature, she represented change in an unchanging environment. She thrived in an environment that valued independence and was unwilling to conform. She was a square peg in a round hole. She was definitely in the wrong place! Had she stayed, she would have been miserable and bitter. Her attitude would have had a terrible impact on her team and the entire program.

NOT THE RIGHT TIME

When a friend of mine finished graduate school, she was ready for another baby. As months started to turn into years, she and her husband felt ignored by God. They couldn't understand why they couldn't get pregnant after surgeries performed by their infertility doctor gave no known reasons for the infertility. They suffered in silence because everyone from family to friends had opinions on how their daughter couldn't be an only child. In the two years they hoped and prayed for a child, there were times when God seemed especially cruel. For instance, when my friend left her gynecologist's office for the last time to pursue their quest for another child with an infertility doctor, she walked out into the waiting room and saw pregnant teenagers. Another time a friend of hers, who was a single mother and was pregnant again, told her she was contemplating an abortion. My friend wondered, "How could God be so cruel to burden my friend with an unplanned pregnancy when I so desperately would love another child?"

After two years of trying to get pregnant, my friend was ready to give up and look at adoption. Her husband was not interested in adoption, so there was tension in the marriage. They did believe God would help them through this situation, so they spent a day praying about it. At the end of the day when they prayed together, God gave them both a different vision of a baby in the near future. Her vision was of her daughter holding a baby, and her husband's vision was of him holding a baby. After those two distinct, yet similar visions, my friend said in confidence that they would have a baby within the year. A year after that prayerful day, they welcomed their second daughter into their family!

It is very hard to accept God's timing at times. My friend wanted a baby when she was ready to have another one. She didn't want to wait. She thought it was the right time to have another child, but God didn't. Many people don't like to accept the fact that they don't always have control over the timing of circumstances. This is a classic time when God becomes the scapegoat for one's anger.

NOT THE RIGHT REASONS

A colleague was plagued by questions about what to do. He had an opportunity to leave a job he had only been at for six months to take a job that would get him out of his unhappy career move. His career path had moved his family around the country six times already and he figured this time would be no different. After hearing negative feedback from his kids and an outside professional telling him his son would not react well to another move, this colleague decided his career path wasn't as important as the welfare of his wife and children.

Whether it wasn't the right place, right time, or right reason, can you relate a life circumstance that fits into one of these categories? If so, then ask yourself, "Did that fuel my sustained anger towards God because something did not work out?"

YOUR LIFE CIRCUMSTANCES

Have you had circumstances in your life where you were almost stunned with how badly a situation or person turned out? Was there an event or situation that was a sure thing, which did not pan out for unforeseen reasons?

All these life experiences bring a cumulative concept of God. You have a choice to become bitter or better from them.

Below is another inventory of possible life circumstances that can negatively impact your view of God. Please put a check next to the items that have applied to your life or add your own:

1. I am divorced.
2. I have (had) a spouse who cheated on me.
3. I am(was) in an abusive marriage/relationship
4. I have(had) rebellious children who have been in trouble with the law.
5. I have been betrayed by friends/family.
6. I have financial problems.
7. I am unhappy in current career/job.
8. I had a business deal fall through.
9. I have a special needs child(ren).
10. I envy other people's success.
11. I often deal with loneliness.
12. I have no one to share my life with.
13. I live with an addict (work, drugs/alcohol, sex, gambling, etc).
14. I have been a victim of sexual assault.
15. There is not one particular trial in my life, just a cumulative bitterness toward God.
16. I have been diagnosed with debilitating illness.
17. I have been diagnosed with terminal illness.
18. I have had negative interactions with "church" people.

NOW WHAT?

So you might have checked off a few items in both your childhood and your life circumstances inventories. I truly believe with awareness comes change. Change might be a very scary idea or one you are ready to embrace. Wherever you are on the continuum, you now have a choice to acknowledge those issues and where they fit in your seasons of life, or ignore them. These circumstances have become the lens in which you filter all other life experiences. If you ignore how these circumstances have impacted you, then your life will continue the way it has been. If that is what you truly wanted, you would not have picked up this book! It is time to put your perceptions in perspective and give yourself the gift of working through all that has held you back for years.

In 1965, The Byrds came out with a song entitled "Turn, Turn, Turn." Some of the lyrics were: *"To everything there is a season, turn, turn, turn. And a time to every purpose under heaven."* That song is actually based on a book in the Bible called Ecclesiastes. These 'times' address the different seasons we will now discuss in the next four chapters. Evaluating the different seasons of your life against the backdrop of your life circumstances will help you discover why God has not been an option in your life.

PART II

SEEING GOD THROUGH YOUR SEASONS OF LIFE

CHAPTER 3

SUMMER - ENJOYING LIFE
TO ITS FULLEST

A time to laugh, a time to dance,
A time to gather stones,
A time to embrace, a time to speak,
A time to love, a time for peace
          --Ecclesiastes, 3 various verses (NIV)

When I was a child, my neighborhood was a great place to live in the summertime. Every day, from morning until evening, the neighborhood "gang" of kids of varying ages would get together and play outdoor games or, when it was raining, play in each others' basements.

As I got older, the hangout became the public pool in our community. Every day, I'd go swimming with the same friends and play the same games and come home tired and hungry from all the energy I burned.

Indicators that you are in a summer season of life:

1. You have a carefree perspective on life.
2. "Negative" situations are seen as 'not so bad.'
3. You are letting go and having more fun.
4. You have lots of energy to tackle projects.
5. You enjoy life and see the positive in everything.
6. You laugh more.
7. You are more relaxed with people and situations.
8. You have higher self-confidence.
9. There is more balance in your life.
10. You no longer allow the stress to get to you.
11. You have a sense of contentment.
12. You give yourself permission to have fun.
13. You experience a sense of peace.

Your summer season is perhaps the easiest time to think of God in a positive light; when life is going well, God is okay. Or, it's a time when you might not even consider God because you're basking in your own glory. The anger enters when life doesn't go quite the way you had planned. Summer becomes a quick skip to winter when you realize you don't have as much control over your life as you think you do.

IS IT SUMMER YET?

Every year around May, my kids start getting antsy for school to be done. The weather is warmer, and they are tired of school. They keep asking, "Isn't it summer yet?"

If you find yourself asking, "Oh, when will life get fun again?" or "When will things slow down?" then you might fall into one of two camps of people: 1) you long to achieve some summer in your life. 2) You are experiencing a summer season and don't want it to end.

I'M READY FOR SUMMER!

The funniest thing I find as a parent is how we parents always say how we'll get the kids together over the summer because there is more time. The reality is that people's schedules get filled with even more activities so that it is almost impossible to set up a day to have friends over. Are you filling up your life with so many activities that it is hard to sit back and actually enjoy them?

If you find yourself longing for a 'summer vacation,' ask yourself, "Are there truly no summer moments in my life, or am I just too busy to notice?"

I have some days that are filled with clients, meetings and networking events. I am tired when I get home. When my girls get home from school, we are either hurrying to do homework or dashing off to extracurricular activities. At dinnertime, we finally sit down and catch our breath to share about our day. It's in those moments of sharing that we stop to enjoy a summer moment in our hectic day. When my husband and I check on the girls before we go to bed, sometimes we'll just stare at them sleeping so peacefully and think about what a blessing they truly are even though we were having tough moments just hours earlier.

How to recognize summer moments in everyday life:

A. You have a sudden shift from a negative to a positive perspective on a person or situation.
B. You sense a release of tension and allow yourself to enjoy the moment you are in.
C. You feel completely content.
D. You decide not to worry about someone (including yourself) or something. Most of what worries us never actually happens.

A SUMMER MOMENT IN OUR COLDEST WINTER

Our youngest daughter, Hannah, was born with heart defects and had three open-heart surgeries by the time she was two years old. She had a big surgery to correct all her heart defects around her second birthday, when we almost lost her due to post-surgery complications. We spent 21 days in the hospital. My summer moment came during that darkest, coldest time came around day 18 when her anti-seizure medication was starting to wear off. The medication had suppressed her small and large motor skills and speech. But on that day when I was holding her on my lap, she fidgeted around until she was facing me (carefully because she still had one chest tube in her), and when I propped her up, she clumsily put her arms around my neck and whispered "Mommy." I cried tears of joy as I rocked her back and forth. It brought me such relief and hope that our baby was coming back to us. I didn't want to let her go. As a mother, I agonized and ached over my inability to hold and comfort her during her cardiac arrests and seizures, but now I had the chance to do what I was unable to do before; I just needed to wait to enjoy those moments.

How about you? Are you waiting to enjoy some summer moments in your life? What could be keeping you from seeing these moments?

Reasons for missing summer moments:

1. Daily schedule packed with too much activity
2. Excessive worry about issues (finances, kids, job, and spouse)
3. Too caught up in others' activities/no time for self
4. No life balance
5. Little or no recognition or unaware of own needs
6. Trying too hard to control everyone and/or everything
7. Performance driven about every aspect of life
8. Expect yourself and others not to make mistakes
9. Life expectations aren't going as planned, too many detours
10. Caught up in own problems, don't see big picture or look at other lives to keep own life in perspective.

As I look over these reasons, I can check off about every item at some point in recent years! Sometimes I wonder if I'm missing out on life because I can become consumed with the day-to-day tasks and demands of all the roles I play in my life.

For those of you enjoying an actual summer season, think about what is making it happen for you: Circumstances? People? Perspective? Even though we'd all like to stay in a summer season forever, it does eventually come to an end. When it does come to an end, whom do you often blame first? You or God? Much of the disappointed population has a tendency to blame God.

Believe it or not, you cycle through the different seasons of life because each season has lessons for you to learn. Whether or not you are ready to learn is not entirely up to you. I believe God wants to partner with you to show the value that each lesson in each season could bring.

Below are some steps to evaluate past or current summer seasons.

STEP 1: THE SITUATION

Describe a current or past summer season in your life. Who is with you? What are you doing? What is your perspective about the situation? The people involved? How do you see yourself? (Confident, happy, purposeful, etc). What is your view of God?

STEP 2: A SEASONAL SHIFT

What changed in your situation that ended your summer season? Was it something you could control? Was there some action or behavior on your part that ended your summer season? What is your view of God during this step?

STEP 3: LIFE APPLICATION

What did you learn about yourself and/or God with this event or moment?

All good things do eventually come to an end. As summer fades into autumn, we will now look at the changes that autumn brings to your life.

CHAPTER 4

AUTUMN - LIFE'S CHANGES

A time to uproot, a time to tear down,
A time to mourn, a time to scatter stones,
A time to refrain, a time to search,
A time to throw away
A time to tear, a time for war
　　　　　--Ecclesiastes, 3 various verses (NIV)

I went to a counseling conference where I attended a workshop on life coaching. I had heard of it years before, but never investigated it. I walked out of the workshop excited to say, "This fits for me. This is what I want to do!" When I got back from the conference, I told my husband Jon I was enrolling in coaching training. I completed my first training program the following February.

At that time I was going through a Bible study that really seemed to be providing the same answers week after week: I was to take a leap of faith and trust God enough to 'retire' from counseling to pursue coaching full-time. "Why would I want to do that?" I asked. "I have a very successful counseling practice with a waiting list, and a steady flow of referrals. Why would I give this up?" The answer that kept coming back was, "There is a whole other world in which to use your talents." So, through a lot of tears and struggle, I decided to slowly wean out of my counseling practice by the end of September, and move on to coaching.

A whole new world opened up to me. My speaking and coaching career is allowing me to work in the business arena, and speak to audiences I never thought possible. I am living outside my comfort zone, but loving every moment of what I do. There is a different kind of passion in the work I do now. Had I not taken that step of faith, I'd be living in my comfort zone and missing a lot of fun people and experiences. I have a new outlook on helping others, one of working with motivated people.

AUTUMN REPRESENTS CHANGE

Change is inevitable. Some people will remain miserable just to avoid change. But for those who are ready, the autumn season brings lessons we need to learn through change. The perspective impacts how you view autumn. You know you are ready to embrace change when you become comfortable with the uncomfortable.

How to tell if you are in an autumn season:

1.   You are in the midst of a life transition (job loss, divorce, etc.).
2.   You're restless (physically, mentally, spiritually).

3. You are looking for changes (in lifestyle, relationships, career, etc.).
4. You think more about future possibilities rather than on current situation.
5. You are 'shedding' your old self (habits, perspectives, approaches to work/life).
6. You are starting a new venture (relationship, business, career, etc.).
7. You are taking action to make changes happen.

YOUR GUT REACTION

When you are making a decision, how do you approach it? Do you write out the pros and cons and gather a lot of information, or do you decide based on your feelings? Has your decision-making process let you down at times?

A gut reaction is when a person says something, or a situation happens, and you know instantly what to do with little thought. Have you ignored that gut reaction at times because you know it means change from what is familiar or comfortable? I have. For instance, when our pediatrician told me the fluid in our two-year old daughter's ears was not affecting her hearing, my gut told me to get a second opinion. It took me months to get that second opinion, but when I took her to an Ear/Nose/Throat specialist who put tubes in her ears, her speech and language development accelerated quickly. There was another time on two separate occasions when a colleague and I were to present a seminar with two different audiences. Circumstances beyond our control cancelled those seminars. I was disappointed we didn't conduct those seminars, but the circumstances confirmed my initial thoughts that I should not work with this colleague. Months later, I found out she was 'making the rounds' to other colleagues to partner in presenting seminars that didn't materialize either. She was only interested in making money, and if the seminars didn't happen, she was on to the next colleague.

How about you? Do you ever have a gut reaction about a person or situation? Is it possible that the gut reaction could be God trying to tell you something? Could God be in that still small voice that says to do or not do something? I have had friends and colleagues tell me that they are not the praying type, but when pressed for a tough decision have found themselves saying, "God, help me out. I need to know what to do."

They fight the fact that they are acknowledging God because they believe themselves to be completely self-sufficient, yet I believe there is deep essence of the soul (not mind or body) that longs to release the burden of self-sufficiency and believe in someone or something else that brings relief to that burden. There is a scripture verse that has helped me at times I was feeling particularly overwhelmed with decisions:

"Take my yoke upon you and learn from me, for I am gentle and humble in heart, and you will find rest for your souls. For my yoke is easy and my burden is light."
Matthew 11:29-30

GETTING THE WIND
KNOCKED OUT OF ME

My CPE (Clinical Pastoral Education) internship was an experience I'll never forget. It was one of two clinical internships required for my graduate program. In CPE, we worked as hospital chaplains where we were assigned certain areas. My areas were the ER and same-day surgery. As part of our full-time summer experience, we were also required to rotate on-call duties.

Within two weeks, my life had turned upside down. Everything I had ever come to believe about people, God, and life went out the window with each chaplain experience I had with a patient, his or her family, or medical staff. It was as if I got the wind completely knocked out of me with no way of gasping to catch a breath. I had completely lost my faith and frame of reference, so I found myself working according to how each situation unfolded. My faith up until that point had provided the air I needed to make decisions. Losing that faith sucked that air out of me.

I lost my faith by having to learn some very hard lessons about myself and the way I worked with people. Twice a week, the other interns and I would discuss and write about our chaplain experiences and how they were affecting us. We were graded by our willingness to accept the challenges of on-call work, deliver sermons to the long-term care facility on Sundays, and be open to the critiques of the supervisor and other interns. Within the first two weeks, my supervisor pounded me with the constant questions like "Why did you do that? How did you know prayer is what that patient needed? Why do you continually shy away from people who react negatively towards a chaplain? What assumptions did you make about this family that kept you from ministering to them they way they would have wanted?" I learned about more insecurities I thought were long gone. I realized I still had a fear of male authority figures, which made me realize through my internship that the God I thought I had come to know and understand was now someone I feared and wasn't interested in understanding. I thought I knew God, but I realized I understood Him from a completely intellectual level and never allowed God to really become personal to me at the heart level because that would mean I would have to be vulnerable. I didn't want to be vulnerable because the internship brought back so many feelings of my childhood abuse. I felt I had no control over how vulnerable I had become because I lost my faith base. That, coupled with the constant examining of why I did what I did, left me feeling numb toward God. My belief system about God and myself spiraled down quicker than I could have possibly believed. I was stunned and shocked. I questioned myself, others, and God on everything. The anger, disappointment, confusion, and pain that I stuffed for so many years came out during my work as a chaplain. I was gripped with thoughts and feelings I never knew existed.

I had a great CPE supervisor who kept challenging me to face the fears and insecurities and break free of them. I wanted to be able to stay in touch with him even after CPE ended. Unfortunately, one week after CPE ended, he died of a massive heart attack while vacationing with his family. His death fueled my anger towards God.

The challenges I faced after CPE were numerous. I still had my second year of seminary to complete, was on staff of a large church, and held another ministry leadership position. How would I get through these obligations while I went through my "dark hour of faith?" I delegated tasks and responsibilities to other leaders, kept my counseling practice to a minimum, laid low while attending seminary classes, and stayed away from well-meaning friends who only wanted to throw scripture at me as a way to combat my rebelliousness. I wanted so desperately to be free from all my responsibilities and do my own thing.

I lived a life completely devoid of God for four months. I stopped praying, attending Bible study, didn't return friends' phone calls, and only went to church because my husband said our daughter needed to see both parents attending church. During those four months, I felt frenzied, depressed, and overwhelmed as I continued to spiral down and away from the faith I had come to know. The burden of self-sufficiency was too much to bear. I became more anxious about everything, felt I was running 100 miles an hour with no time to stop and breathe, and felt no sense of direction or peace. I was exhausted after four months of running away.

It was at my seminary's Christmas program that I was asked to speak about a gift that I was thankful for. There, in front of all of my colleagues and other students, I shared some of my painful journey over the past few months. I told them how I had to take a hard look at what I had become in sharing faith with others: I came across arrogant and trite; I learned how much I tried to control other people's feelings and thoughts by glossing it over with prayer and clichés; and I needed to be completely separated from God for a time in order to see how much I really wanted and needed Him in my life. During my months of separation from God, even though my heart and mind were far away from Him, I believe I was protected from making some really poor choices. For example, even though I loved my husband dearly, I wanted to take off and leave because he represented a faith I wanted no part of; I wanted to leave seminary and forget my graduate degree; I so desperately just wanted to take off from life for a while and go hide away where no one could find me and I was free of responsibilities. I had been burdened with having to be so responsible from the age of three that I resented God for making that burden so heavy. What my time off from God showed me was that I placed a lot of that burden on myself. My recovery work as an Adult Child of an Alcoholic showed me that my value and worth came from taking on responsibilities that would allow me to feel good about myself and that I was contributing to the world.

Somehow I managed to talk through my tears. My CPE experience was the gift that I cherished at that moment. As I sat back down, we sang "Silent Night." The tears continued to come, and in that moment, I felt that I had run back into God's arms. The marathon I ran for four months was grueling, and I was glad to finally cross the finish line. I collapsed in sheer exhaustion, but I was ever so grateful that the marathon turned me into a strong runner.

Those four months brought many changes I had no clue were coming. Those changes were:

1. I saw I could make a fresh, new start with God and build a new foundation for how I would approach and view Him; my approach with God is now heartfelt, and my views built against the backdrop of the Bible and how it is applied in my life and lives of others.

2. I saw people struggling with their faith in a whole new light. I have learned to meet people where they are and not inflict my agenda onto their lives.

3. My CPE experience put me back into counseling and allowed me to approach support groups, by seeking what I needed to learn about myself and *not* just worrying about how to help others. I took responsibility for my own recovery and learned to release a lot of the shame I believed about myself for so many years.

4. I was very open to learning about whom I was and why I was here. A book that helped me tremendously to see myself through God's

eyes rather than my shame-based past was "Victory Over the Darkness" by Neil Anderson. Shame-based is defined as believing "I am what's wrong" rather than "I did something wrong." See the difference? For so many years I believed I, as a person, was wrong. I never separated myself as a person from my behaviors and actions. My alcoholic/abusive background taught me they were one in the same. But the book taught me they are separate! I learned for the first time how to see myself in a positive rather than negative light. I experienced a huge paradigm shift. I felt as if the weight of the world had been lifted off my shoulders, and I was now free to experience my life the way God intended it to be lived. I have a confidence in myself that I was unable to experience the first 27 years of my life. There are people and circumstances that challenge that confidence at times, but thankfully I am able to resort to the truth and comfort of what the Bible says I am. Until that paradigm shift, my confidence was based on what others thought of me and how well I performed in situations.

There is a children's book by well-known author Max Lucado titled "You Are Special." Even though it was a gift for my daughters, I have used it at many speaking engagements over the years because it beautifully illustrates this concept of seeing yourself through God's eyes.

It's the story of a town of wooden people called the Wemmicks. In this town, the Wemmicks go around giving each other stars and dots. The stars are for people who look good or are outgoing and involved in the town's happenings. The dots are for the introverts, and people who are not as involved. Punchinello, an, introvert, is covered with dots, and the other Wemmicks covered with stars look down at him and say mean things.

Punchinello meets a girl named Lucia who has no stars or dots on her wooden body. Intrigued, Punchinello asks Lucia how she is able to be free of stars or dots. She explains that she goes to visit the wood maker at the top of the hill every day. The wood maker tells her how special she is and that what the other Wemmicks think doesn't matter. Punchinello decides to visit this wood maker because he doesn't want the dots anymore.

When he visits the wood maker, he is surprised to see how gentle the wood maker is in talking to him. Punchinello figured the wood maker would make fun of him like the other Wemmicks did, but he didn't. The wood maker notices all the dots but tells Punchinello that the dots only stick if he lets them. In other words, if Punchinello truly believes what others say about him, then he will feel as low as they put him. But if Punchinello were to come visit the wood maker daily, then he could learn how truly special he really is. The Wemmicks were made out of the same wood. Why were they any different from Punchinello? What mattered most was what the wood maker thought, and he thought Punchinello was special. As Punchinello left the wood maker's house, a dot fell off his wooden body because he also started to believe he was special.

Can you relate to this story? On what are you basing your self-worth? Do you feel covered with dots like Punchinello? Are you willing to start seeing yourself through God's eyes? If so, would that change your view of God? Sometimes, whether you are ready or not, change inevitably comes. Your autumn season can bring necessary changes that can move you forward, perhaps out a rut you have been in for a very long time.

I'M EXPERIENCING AUTUMN RIGHT NOW!

If you find yourself in the midst of change, what is helping you navigate through it? What is your compass? Consider asking yourself the following questions:

1. Am I open to this change? (If not, you will most likely view this situation through more of a 'negative lens.')
2. Will I view it as a learning experience or an unappreciated life interruption?

Some of the work our coaching firm does is with people in career transition. These transitions are often unplanned. Some people are not very open to the changes that career transition brings and how it impacts their career goals and family life. Others use their transition as a time of learning and exploring what they truly want in their personal and professional lives. It is often a time of re-evaluating priorities.

Consider filtering your autumn situation through the steps below. I will use my CPE experience as an example:

STEP 1: THE SITUATION

These would be the facts about you, others and the actual event. NO PERCEPTIONS, FACTS ONLY. Then include your perception of God at the end of this step.

1. I worked as a chaplain for 10 weeks in the summer of 1995.
2. I was assigned the ER, same-day surgery, and on-call responsibilities.
3. Lost my faith within two weeks of starting the internship.
4. Supervisor dies one week after CPE ends.

PERCEPTION OF GOD: Numb. I can't feel anything. I want no part of God.

STEP 2: AERIAL VIEW OF SITUATION

Now look beyond the event. What do you notice about others involved in the situation? What else is happening surrounding the event? What are your thoughts and feelings about the event or moments? What else do you notice about the event? What was said or done to or for you? List all positive or negative. Include your perception of God at the end of this step.

Positive:
1 The learning environment promoted a lot of self-reflection to see my strengths and weaknesses in helping others.
2 Had a supervisor who challenged me to break out of my comfort zone to broaden my scope of expertise.
3 Had a lot of fun working with fellow CPE students.
4 Had a very supportive husband during a very difficult time.
5 I learned a tremendous amount of how NOT to minister to people in a hospital setting.
6 My CPE experience significantly changed my life.

Negative:

1 Losing my faith put me in a tailspin where I had no direction or point of reference in which to minister to people in the chaplain context.

2 My confusion, anger and distrust toward God put a lot of stress on my marriage.

3 My husband worried whether I'd find my way back to God and how that would impact our marriage. Our relationship with God was the foundation of our marriage.

4 I was scared I wouldn't return to God. If I didn't have a faith, how would I live my life? Where would my hope come from?

5 My CPE supervisor was the first male authority figure I ever trusted or respected. When he died suddenly, it fueled my anger towards God because He took away someone I was willing to trust for the first time in my life.

6 Long hours, tough on-call nights left me emotionally and physically drained for the entire summer. I had little or no energy left for my husband or daughter.

7 Received some very negative reactions from patients and/or family when I introduced myself as a chaplain.

PERCEPTION OF GOD: Distant, uninvolved and angry with God. God was a blank slate to me. I didn't care and didn't want to understand anything about God. I was in full rebellion.

STEP 3: THIRD PERSON VIEW OF SITUATION

Now view your situation as an outsider. What does this outsider say about your situation? What do you notice? Is there anything that should be added or changed concerning the situation? Compare yourself to a person in a similar situation.

Peeling the layers of an onion can be painful. As you get to the core of the onion, the pungent smell brings tears to your eyes. There is no way to stop the tears from coming.

CPE represented the layers (years of my life) being peeled back to reveal the true core and essence on which I built my life. Those layers protected me from pain, hurt, anger and confusion that in the end failed me.

I ran. I rebelled. I didn't want the tears to come. The more I tried to run, the more confused and chaotic my life became. Even though I pushed God away, I sensed that He was always there waiting for me to return.

PERCEPTION OF GOD: Protected me even when I ran away by keeping me from leaving my husband, leaving graduate school and running away where no one could find me for a while. I felt far away from God, although He was not far from me.

STEP 4: RE-EVALUATE SITUATION

Has your perspective now changed? Do you see yourself, others, the situation or God any differently? Can any of the positives you listed be God working "behind the scenes?"

God was there waiting for me. I am reminded of the parable of the Prodigal son in the New Testament. A young son decides he wants his piece of inheritance from his father so he can go off and squander his money as he sees fit. He has lots of fun and friends, but when his money runs out, so do his fun times and friends. He is reduced to eating the pig feed in troughs for food. He realizes that his father's servants back home eat better than he does. He decides to return home, not knowing if his father will even allow him to come back.

Much to this son's surprise, his father welcomes him with open arms and even throws him a welcome home party because the father is so glad to have his son back home.

My seminary's Christmas program is when I ran back into God's open arms. I was glad to be back home after months in the desert wandering and lost on my own. I realized I needed to be without God in order to see how much I really needed Him.

PERCEPTION OF GOD: Loving, faithful to me even when I wasn't.

STEP 5: LIFE APPLICATION

What did you learn about yourself and/or God with this event or moment?

I learned that no matter how rebellious I was, God was watching over me and protecting me. I realized after I quit running just how much God really loved me to protect me from that disastrous road my rebellious spirit wanted to take.

CHAPTER 5

WINTER - LIFE'S COLD SPELLS

A time to die, a time to kill,
A time to weep, a time to mourn,
A time to give up, a time to hate,
A time to be silent.
Ecclesiastes, 3 various verses (NIV)

Now I realize that you might live in a climate that never sees snow. To you, your winter might be 60 degrees with lots of rain. Whatever your winter may be, imagine the worst weather conditions you have experienced and store that in your mind for your winter analogy.

DRIVING THROUGH A SNOW STORM

My family and I decided to drive back early after spending Thanksgiving in Chicago. We didn't check the weather before we left, and by the time we reached the mid-section of Michigan, we ran into a blizzard. It seemed to come out of nowhere, and we soon found ourselves driving at a snail's pace with almost zero visibility. The salt trucks had not plowed through yet, so none of the cars knew where the lanes or shoulders of the road where. We drove for what seemed like forever, but as we continued, we drove where salt trucks and plows had been. And then, as quickly as we entered into the blizzard, we entered the part of the state that had no snow. We were relieved to drive the rest of the way home safely.

What do you think or do when a life 'storm' with zero visibility hits you? Have those storms looked like a death of a loved one, a divorce, job loss, or cancer diagnosis? Were you able to see the storm coming, or did it come out of nowhere? Often times, a winter season will take you by surprise because your life might have been too busy to notice. You assume life is okay and can resent when an interruption occurs. That resentment is often towards God. It's a human response. If God has not been a part of your life, why is He the first thing you blame when life goes wrong? Admit it or not, there is your spiritual side!

Indicators you're in a winter season:
1. You have a negative view of self.
2. You have a negative view of others.
3. You have a negative view of a particular situation.
4. You blame God for your circumstances.
5. Your bitterness/anger toward God continues to grow.

6. You see no hope for your situation to get better.

If you checked off two or more bullet points, you are currently in a winter season.

IT WAS A BAD YEAR

The year 2001 was definitely a tough year for me. In January, I became Power of Attorney for my ailing mother, and had to move her from independent living to a nursing home. She lived in Chicago, so I had to plan a few days to tour nursing facilities and make decisions with her. Friends helped me clean out her apartment, which allowed me to set up details with the nursing home and get her finances in order. All of that in four days! I was exhausted!

In March, our daughter Hannah had her second open-heart surgery. She was seven months old, and they were supposed to do the "big" surgery to correct all her heart defects, but the surgeon decided on the table not to perform it because Hannah had an allergic reaction to the bypass medication. Instead, they put in a central shunt to tide her over for another year until she could handle the bigger surgery. The shunt was very large, so she had a two-month recovery as she struggled with symptoms of congestive heart failure until she grew more into her shunt. The stress of being a diligent parent for her care was at times overwhelming.

In May, three days after moving into our new house (that was the only event that went smoothly!), I received a call from an oncologist in Chicago telling me my mom's swollen arm turned out to be cancer and that she only had about six weeks to live. The cancer had spread to her lymph nodes and other organs, so there was nothing that could be done. No one told my mother she had cancer, so when I went to the hospital the next day, I gave her the news. She was in shock and didn't say much. I stayed with her for a while until other family members showed up. I had to close her bank accounts, make hospice arrangements, and plan her funeral. Luckily, my brother joined me at the funeral home in making arrangements. I was sad, yet relieved. My mother was so unhappy her whole life. She lived life as if she were an empty shell ever since I was born. The life she hated was almost over.

My mother died six weeks to the day of her diagnosis. Others were devastated that she went so quickly. I again was relieved that she didn't have to suffer long. If you have watched someone die from cancer, you know how difficult it is for the patient and the family. My mom never could endure pain of any kind-whether it was emotional or physical. Her alcoholism was her comfort and escape from pain for so many years. She was finally free from that pain that she had inflicted on herself.

I was sad to have lost my mom; we were never close, but I continue to grieve over the loss of a dream. The dream of a mother/daughter relationship that I only hope can now be built with my three daughters. I can never be my mother's daughter again.

A CLOSE CALL WITH DEATH, TWICE

In August 2002, Hannah had her third open heart surgery in her young, two-year life. This was the 'big' surgery that had been delayed. In-laws came to help and be with us for more than a week, which helped us tremendously.

Hannah's surgery went smoothly which was a relief. We knew from her two previous surgeries that successful surgery is just the first hurdle to overcome in recovery.

Complications started occurring within 24 hours after surgery. Her heart was tachycardic (rapid heart beat) and her blood pressure was dropping. The doctor told us that he couldn't guarantee she'd make it through the night. Maybe it was denial or mother's instinct, but I knew Hannah was a bigger fighter than that. She wouldn't give up so easily. We stayed at the Ronald McDonald house across the street from the hospital, but had a restless sleep, anticipating a dreaded call from ICU.

We made it through the night, and Hannah was stabilized for the next day. On her third post surgery day, the real trouble began. My husband Jon had a meeting at work that was the only obligation he had to fulfill that week, and I was going over to the hospital after having lunch across the street. When I got to the waiting area, I didn't notice that all visitors were out there. (An indication that there is a child in trouble and everyone is requested to leave the unit so as not to upset other parents). I called in to come back to see Hannah when a nurse informed me that Hannah went into cardiac arrest and they were trying to get her back. They told me to come back to the holding room where a doctor would come to talk to me. I was met by a social worker who told me that they couldn't get a hold of my husband on his cell phone. (The one time he had his phone shut off!). They tried calling our home where grandparents were, but our home phone for some reason was not working, so they had to call a neighbor to go over to our house and inform the grandparents what was occurring. They also called our church and had one of the pastors come.

In those moments as I waited completely alone for the doctor to give me news, I wondered why this all had to happen. It was almost surreal. The doctor came back and told me that they got her back after ten minutes of CPR, drugs and paddles to shock her heart back into rhythm. My first words to her when I saw her were "Hannah, don't do this. Don't scare us like that. Stay with us."

When Jon finally called in, he said. "Just tell me, is she alive or dead?"

"She's alive, she's okay. They got her back. Just drive carefully. She's stabilized for now."

Jon and the pastor got to the hospital around the same time, just a short time before shift change for the nurses. Right as we were leaving for shift change, Hannah went into cardiac arrest AGAIN! We went back to the same holding room and waited to hear what was going on. By the time the doctor came back to see us five minutes later, Hannah was back again. The doctor felt she indeed was now stabilized. Just for good measure, they kept the unit's crash cart (materials needed to provide CPR, medications, and paddles) right by her bed.

I lived in crisis mode for the rest of Hannah's hospital stay. There was good reason. Twenty-four hours after her first cardiac arrest, Hannah started having seizures. Her first one occurred during shift change, so we couldn't see her. They rushed her down for a CT scan to check if she was having a stroke, and by the time shift change was over, she was back. Jon and I went back to the Ronald McDonald house during shift change and cried and prayed. I was angry at God as I prayed and said, "God, wasn't yesterday enough? We almost lost her twice yesterday, and now this? If she strokes out, what would be left of her? Yesterday's only reassurance was that she would still have her faculties, and now you're scaring us with this? God, please don't let this happen!"

Her CT scan showed brain swelling, but no stroke. They couldn't explain the brain swelling, except that it might have been from the chest compressions from the prior day's CPR. An EEG was scheduled for the next day to see what might be causing the seizures. Hannah had two more seizures that day, each one longer in duration. It is an absolute horrible feeling to watch a child seize and be completely helpless to help. They had Hannah completely drugged up with morphine (pain killer) and Phenobarbital (anti-seizure) to keep her still so she could recuperate from all her trauma.

The large doses she received would prove to be another obstacle for her and for us in her recovery. The Phenobarbital suppressed her appetite, speech, and physical movement. We had no way of knowing if her limitations were from the seizures and cardiac arrests or the medicine. Watching her withdrawal from the large doses of narcotics was a nightmare. Her inability to eat or sleep did not help her recovery. They had her on a feeding tube, but when they increased her feeding, she threw up. If we tried to feed her, she'd refuse or would throw up if she ate too much. I insisted she have something to help take the edge off of the withdrawal. It is cruel to see a child withdraw from drugs without any help.

Sometimes it may feel like the hell on earth will never end. It can, in fact, end, even if circumstances don't change. A shift in your perspective can help you start seeing spring moments in your darkest times.

Hannah started to emerge out of her "winter" season as she began weaning down on her Phenobarbital and more of her personality started to return. When she was released from the hospital 21 days later, her recovery skyrocketed, and her physical and developmental capabilities returned.

SPRING MOMENTS DURING WINTER SEASONS

Living in the Midwest, I love it when we get a 70-degree day in mid-February. It gives me hope that spring will indeed come, and I won't have to endure winter forever.

When you are in a winter season of life, is the snowstorm blinding you so you cannot possibly see any hope of coming out of it? Or do you see the sun starting to peak through the clouds and the snow stopping?

For some of you, you are in your deepest, darkest season right now and see no way out. Life or the situation seems hopeless. I can understand that. I find that if I wallow in the problems and the hopelessness of the situation, I have tunnel vision, and don't see a light at the end of the tunnel. The tunnel becomes never ending. I have found, in retrospect, that often I create my own tunnel through perpetual negative thoughts, feelings and sometimes actions. I start assuming everything is going wrong, so why bother? I create my own vacuum. If you find yourself in this spiral or have in the past, take heed. Misery is an option. You can choose to develop a better perspective in order to live and learn through your winter seasons.

My years as a therapist showed me that often times people are easily shut down when a cold front moves through. It is as if they live in the Midwest, yet don't plan on buying a winter jacket because they figure they won't need it. Unless they want to freeze to death, they eventually have to buy a coat in order to survive the winter. Survival skills for your winter season could look like preparing your car for winter travel:

1. *Keep food, water, and blankets in your trunk in case you get stranded.* You can't always depend on your cell phone because it might not have a signal! Be aware of how to keep your basic needs met while 'stranded' in your winter season. Often times the stress of a crisis keeps people from eating and sleeping properly. If the basics are ignored, it truly does impact your ability to make effective decisions.

2. *Keep chains for your tires/utilize your 4x4 when your driving on ice.* Before utilizing my 4x4 Jeep on ice, I am cautious, almost fearful about losing control of the vehicle. After I shift into greater traction, I gain a little more confidence that I am not going to slide or crash into another car. Your chains or 4x4 could be the existing support system you utilize when tough times hit. Do you have friends or family you can talk to who will challenge you to learn something from your winter season? Or do you surround yourself with yes people who will always tell you what you want to hear, but not necessarily what you need to hear?

3. *Have a cell phone handy in case you get in an accident.* The trick is to avoid an accident. But if you do get in trouble, do you truly have only yourself to rely on? Can you call for help from God? In your desperation, can you pray to God? Believing and knowing you can call on something other than yourself can bring much needed relief from your accident.

4. *Keep a shovel in your trunk:* These are the actual problem solving skills you will need to dig yourself out of a 'snow bank' in your winter season.

Ask yourself:
A. How did I get here?
B. What is my responsibility for getting stuck?
C. What ideas do I have to contribute to solve this? Can I ask for others input?
D. What are my best options?
E. What is my first step to resolving this issue?
F. What action steps am I willing to take after my first step?

WHAT IS A SPRING MOMENT IN YOUR WINTER SEASON?

A spring moment is a break in the negativity of a situation. It can be experienced during or after. It is when you get a glimpse of hope, a shift in perspective, or sudden moment of reality about your situation.

Examples of spring moments in a winter season might be:
1. You no longer need radiation treatment because your tumor shrank to a tiny size.
2. Your soon-to-be ex-spouse is cooperative during divorce proceedings.
3. You land a job after being unemployed for a year.
4. You pay off one of your large credit card bills.
5. Your teenager has decided to start talking to you again.

What might be some of your spring moments in your winter seasons? Include your past and present experiences below.

EVALUATING YOUR WINTER SEASONS

Before we start evaluating, there is a pre-step to consider. First, evaluate your mind and heart. Are you truly ready and willing to look at these situations, and allow yourself to consider a different perspective? If not, ask yourself why. Will you choose bitterness or hope? Evaluation has given me freedom from myself. When I have been resistant to examine my winter season, I have found my pride gets in the way because I don't want to have to admit that I might have contributed to it! It's time to get over yourself and move on!

EXAMINE YOUR WINTER SEASONS/MOMENTS

The following steps will help you journey through your darkest times. I will use our experience with Hannah's third surgery as an example. You might want to grab a pad of paper or hop on your computer to write out your steps. I suggest doing these steps when you have a block of time available with no distractions.

STEP 1: THE SITUATION

These would be the facts about you, others and the actual event. NO PERCEPTIONS, FACTS ONLY. Then include your perception of God at end of this step.

1. Hannah's third surgery
2. Complications starting 24 hours post-op
3. Two cardiac arrests three days post-op
4. Seizures four days post-op
5. Withdrawal from narcotics that kept her from eating on her own or sleeping for four days

6. Last chest tube (out of three) developing an air bubble which had to be removed before ready
7. Hannah, a two-year old with the physical movements of a seven-month old
8. Hannah spending her second birthday in ICU
9. Hannah spending 21 days in the hospital

PERCEPTION OF GOD: Cruel, demanding

STEP 2: AERIAL VIEW OF SITUATION

Now look beyond the event. What do you notice about others involved in the situation? What else is happening surrounding the event moments? What are your thoughts and feelings towards the event or moments? What else do you notice about the event? What was said or done to or for you? List all positive or negative. Include your perception of God at the end of this step.

POSITIVE
1 Hannah is alive. Had she had the surgery when it was originally planned when she was seven months old, she'd be dead.
2 In-laws were there to take care of Hannah's sisters and home while we were living at the hospital.
3 Friends, neighbors, church provided meals for a month.
4 Hannah and we were on prayer lists around the nation – teams of people diligently praying.
5 Neighbors, friends took care of older sisters after in-laws left.
6 After seizures, there were no more traumatic events.
7 EEG's showed no seizure activity.

8   As Hannah slowly came down on seizure medication dosage, more of her original self began to return.

9   She came off the ventilator the day before her birthday.

10 The seizures were NOT a stroke.

11 Hannah was able to hug me and whisper "Mommy" 18 days post-op.

12 I was able to hold Hannah nine days post-op.

13 Her last chest tube and the air bubble did not cause any complications. She was able to go home two days later.

14 Friends and neighbors joined us for a welcome home party for Hannah.

15 As Jon and I slowly weaned Hannah from her seizure medication, Hannah continued to return to us. Once the Phenobarbital was completely out of her system (three weeks post-op), Hannah was restored to her original state.

16 Walking was restored three weeks post-op.

NEGATIVE

1   We had to watch Hannah's withdrawal from the morphine and Phenobarbital.

2   We watched Hannah have seizures and go into cardiac arrest.

PERCEPTION OF GOD: Traumatic events, but He provided for and protected Hannah and us. He has given us a fighter and a strong-willed child whom we wouldn't trade for anything!

STEP 3: THIRD PERSON VIEW OF SITUATION

Now view your situation as an outsider. What does this outsider say about your situation? What do you notice? Is there anything that should be added or changed concerning the situation? How would this compare to a person in a similar situation?

One very important fact I have learned through all our hospital stays with Hannah, is that there is always another child that is sicker than she. Just when I'm ready to get bitter or down, there is a new child or situation that puts me into perspective and I think, "I need to be grateful for what we have."

STEP 4: RE-EVALUATE SITUATION

Has your perspective now changed? Do you see yourself, others, the situation or God any differently? Can any of the positives you listed be God working "behind the scenes?"

Yes, absolutely to all the above questions. My perspective changed in several different realms:

1. I no longer take life for granted. I live each day appreciating not only Hannah's life, but everyone's I hold so dear, including my own.
2. I have developed a much stronger faith in God coming through Hannah's surgeries. There were obvious miracles that stepped in where science and medicine ended.
3. I see God as even more faithful as I did before because of the way He provided strength and wisdom during the coldest season of our lives. He protected her life even before this last surgery by her allergic reaction to heart bypass

medication at her seven month surgery. That allergy bought the necessary time needed to insure she would live.

4. I see that we all have a specific purpose here on earth. Hannah's purpose is to show God's love, care, compassion, protection and provision to those who might feel helpless or hopeless.

5. I learned the difficult lesson that control is but an illusion. As I sat helplessly watching Hannah seize, go into cardiac arrest, and withdrawal from pain medication, I realized how little I really control.

STEP 5: LIFE APPLICATION

What did you learn about yourself and/or God with this event or moment?

The book of Esther is the only one in the Old Testament that does not have God speaking to His people or blatantly showing His miracles. Queen Esther is actually a woman of Jewish descent, although King Xerxes of Persia doesn't know that. By winning favor with the king, she is able to thwart the plan the king's aide Haman had to rid Persia of its Jewish nation living inside its borders. Queen Esther was strategically placed "for such a time as this" (Esther 4: 14b) to alert the king of the plot against the Jews. Her Jewish nation was spared the fate Haman tried to inflict. After reading the book, one can see how God worked 'behind the scenes' to reveal His care, love and protection for those He loves. Sometimes I wonder if I expect God to reveal and help through a situation with a crash of thunder and lightning bolt. Instead, I have had to learn to keep my eyes and ears open before, during, and after a winter season so that I can see that God was working even before the 'storm' occurred.

This was evident in Hannah's surgery situation. In May, three months before Hannah's surgery, Jon and I were having so many doubts that Hannah would survive this surgery. We worried, and had nightmares, but tried not to buy into them, because we wanted to have faith that God would protect and provide as He did during the other two surgeries.

It was a Friday afternoon in May when my older daughters were at school and Hannah was down for a nap. I was in our basement family room having some quiet time with God, and as I was praying, my thoughts turned negative. I played out a scenario in my mind of Hannah going into cardiac arrest, and the doctors being unable to save her. I started crying because I was able to picture the scene of what ICU room she was in, (I was familiar with the ICU setup from Hannah's previous surgeries) the three doctors and nurses in there trying to resuscitate her, and where I was standing outside the room watching all the activity. As I continued to watch the doctors, I said to myself "God, please let me take her place. Don't let her suffer like this." I continued in that scenario to her funeral: where it would be, what would be said, who would be there, etc. As I was thinking about the funeral, out of nowhere, I very clearly heard God's voice say, "Lynn, that is not the plan I have for her." I was stunned, yet after those words were said, my worry and fear left me, never to return. When my husband Jon came home from work that day, I told him what happened, and in a reassuring, assertive voice I said, "Hannah is going to be fine."

You might be thinking, "I don't really have a connection with God. How would I know if He were talking to me? What do I look for?" Here are a few questions to ask yourself that could help you make a connection:

1. Ask yourself, "Am I really willing and open to hear what God has to say about this situation?"

2. If you pray, do you give God a shopping list of requests and expect answers to those prayers immediately? If so, your approach to God might be that of taking, and not giving. A relationship takes two. You expect God to be meeting your requests, not your needs. Believing that God, not people and circumstances, can meet your needs is a first step to hearing Him and building a one-on-one relationship with Him.

3. Do you trust that God does speak to those who seek out His wisdom?

4. Can you sit still and block out the world for at least five minutes to actually listen for comforting words, a scripture verse or see a visual picture in your mind that gives you peace and comfort? God will communicate with you the way you can understand and receive it. It is different for every person.

5. God doesn't always speak in the quiet moments. He can use other people or situations to speak to you. As a person is talking, certain words can grab your attention that is a message for you to hear. After a situation occurs, a sudden reflection back to a particular part provides a 'pearl of wisdom' that stirs more reflection for you. If you're willing to keep your eyes and ears open, God could speak to you on a daily basis.

When I was alone in the ICU's holding room, awaiting news about Hannah after her first cardiac arrest, hearing God's voice prior to her surgery is what gave me confidence and peace that although the circumstances looked grim for her survival, I knew better. The social worker commented on how calm I was through this crisis. I knew my choice was, I could either trust the circumstances or trust God. God prepared me ahead of time for this crisis when I almost lost my daughter. I am forever grateful and thankful that He did. That strength carried me through a harrowing experience.

STEP 5: LIFE APPLICATION

What did you learn about yourself and/or God with this event or moment?

The biggest lesson I had to learn was that control is just an illusion. There were many people and situations I believed I could control over the years when in reality I was forced to see that being human meant I couldn't change what I couldn't control. The helpless feelings of watching my daughter suffer and struggle for life humbled me. The hardest thing to do was let go of the control.

In thinking about what I wrote in Step 4, you might be wondering, "Well, that's great that God prepared you ahead of time for the outcome of Hannah's surgery, but what about when He doesn't?" God might not speak to you directly, but in evaluating your winter moments, were there 'warning signs' or flashing red lights you might have chosen to ignore? For example, physical symptoms you ignored initially and later turned into a heart attack or cancer? A spouse telling you there are problems, but you ignore the problems until suddenly confronted with divorce.

What about those winter times that truly gives no warning? A child dies of SIDS, a loved one dies in a car crash, or a simple fall down the stairs leaves you paralyzed. During those moments as well, we often respond with great sadness and anger. Rightfully so. How do you reconcile an event that completely alters your life as you know it?

I believe it starts with acknowledging the great loss. With that great loss, comes the grieving. The grieving process looks like:

1. *Shock*. Life is in slow motion-the tragedy almost seems surreal.
2. *Denial*. No, it can't be. It really didn't happen.
3. *Anger*. How could this happen? My great life is no longer!
4. *Healing*. I'm willing to let go and move through the pain and resentment.
5. *Acceptance*. I'm willing to move on and have learned life lessons as a result of this tragedy. I accept my new life after this loss.

Healing and acceptance will be discussed in the spring chapter, but for now, let's focus on shock, denial, and anger. These are most associated with a winter season. There is no set time frame as to how long you would spend in each step of the grieving process. One person's shock might last for a few days, while another person might be stunned for months or years. There is no formula to follow which will hurry you through each step because each individual has his or her own unique process. This process begins for each person when you are able to acknowledge you have suffered a loss. A loss left unrecognized leads to a negative view that can keep you bound to an unhappy, unhealthy life.

For example, growing up in the alcoholic, abusive home that I did, I could have tried to ignore the impact it had on me and assume I could live a 'normal' life once I no longer lived under that roof. My physical environment changed, but my perception of everyone and everything had not. When I became engaged is when I realized I needed to address how my childhood could impact my marriage and future. I enrolled in an Adult Children of Alcoholics support group on my college campus. After a semester, I thought I was 'cured' of my past. Little did I know that the first ACoA group would be just the tip of the iceberg in terms of how my past really was impacting my decision-making process, my (in)ability to trust others, and my need to control people and situations. Even if I wanted to, I couldn't ignore my past's impact because I was living out the impact everyday.

I was in two car accidents within a year in which I was a passenger. Both crashes occurred exactly the same way, so both times I suffered from whiplash. I figured I was fine because I didn't need any medical attention. Problems with my neck and back started occurring six years after these car crashes. My chiropractor educated me about what happens to muscles when left to heal incorrectly. My visits were due to what happened years before. Left unchecked, incorrect healing can lead to more long-term damage.

It seems easier to ignore the pain than to take the time to let something heal. Ways to ignore past pain include addictions, busyness, or focusing all attention on helping others rather than taking care of yourself. Do you see how the cycle begins? It starts with a loss unrecognized or unacknowledged that leads to an unhealthy lifestyle in an attempt to ignore the loss, which leads to more loss and resentment. It's a never-ending cycle if you decide to 'spin your wheels' in hopes that trying something or someone different will get you to a different destination. In all your efforts, you find your bitterness and resentment grows. Instead of taking responsibility, it's easier to blame God for your present circumstances.

READY TO ACKNOWLEDGE THE LOSS

If you are at a point of willingness to see your tragedy as a loss and move through it, you are demonstrating your courage! This is a huge first step. Put your kid gloves on, and treat yourself gently as you walk through this journey. You might find yourself or others saying that you should do this, or shouldn't think that. Stop 'shoulding' on yourself. Say to yourself, "I will not 'should' on myself today!" Say it out loud and often if you need to.

Exercise:
1. Examine the four steps you have done with your winter seasons. Go through one step at a time.
2. Now, take the five steps of the grieving process and see if you can write down where these steps fit in each winter season evaluation. For example, shock could go along with your first step of facts about the situation. NOTE: You might not be able to identify all five grieving steps in your winter seasons.
3. For the winter events where there is no healing or acceptance, identify and write down what action step you are willing to take to get unstuck from your anger phase (i.e. counseling, support group or reconciling with someone).
4. Ask a trusted person to hold you accountable to that action step or plan.

5. Follow through on your action plan as soon as possible. If you wait more than twenty-four hours to do something, you most likely won't follow through.
6. If you are having trouble with your action plan, identify and write a list of benefits that will occur when you move forward to the healing and acceptance stages. This list of benefits will help you see that your life and outlook on it can be different!

I'M STUCK IN THE ANGER PHASE

"Be kind to each other, tenderhearted, forgiving one another, just as God through Christ has forgiven you."
Ephesians 4:32

You might find that you can't seem to move beyond the anger stage. The ability to move out of the anger stage and into healing and acceptance requires a look at forgiveness. What or whom do you need to forgive? Do you need to forgive yourself or others for having been in a winter season?

In Neil Anderson's "Victory Over the Darkness," he beautifully addresses what forgiveness is and is not.

1. Forgiveness is a pardon. Pardon means erasing their offense (never use it against them). Forgiveness does *not* mean forgetting. Forgetting may be the result of forgiveness, but it is never the means of forgiveness. Even God in his omniscience, cannot forget. God remembers our sins no more.
2. Forgiveness is a choice, a crisis of the will. This is difficult because it runs counter to our sense of justice. We want revenge. You might say, "They don't deserve to be let off the hook.

You don't know how much they hurt me." But you need to forgive for your own sake, so you can be free. Your need to forgive isn't an issue between you and the other person; it is between you and God.

3. You'll live with the consequences of the other person's bad choices. Your choice is to do it in the bitterness of unforgiveness or the freedom of forgiveness.

4. Learn to forgive from your heart. How do you do that? You acknowledge the hurt and the hate. Forgiveness is incomplete unless you let it visit your emotional core.

5. Don't wait to forgive until you feel like forgiving; you will never get there. Freedom from the bitterness and resentment is what will be gained.

You might be saying, "These steps are *a lot* easier said than done." I can relate to that. I thought I had forgiven my mother until seeing her in a hospital bed not knowing if she would live or die. It took almost losing her to get it through my thick skull that had she died, I would have regretted not telling her I forgave her.

I have worked with many people over the years that carried the burden of regret and unforgiveness. They live their lives as if they are a car stuck in mud, perpetually spinning its wheels, only to find them digging deeper into the mud. Without forgiveness, you will find yourself "stuck" in your winter season perpetually trying to spin your wheels out of the rut, only to question why you are unable to enjoy any spring or summer moments in your life.

If the concept of forgiveness is still completely foreign and you might be getting angry just thinking about it, then it has hit a nerve for you. May I suggest not ignoring this important piece, but seek out avenues to help you work through it.

Ways to work towards forgiveness: (Writing your responses down has more impact than just thinking about them.)

1. Be willing to verbalize why you are angry with that person or persons.
2. What are the benefits to you to continue with your unforgiveness?
3. Can you truly be honest with yourself and say that your unforgiveness is *not* impacting your other relationships? (When I couldn't forgive my mom, I couldn't forgive anyone who hurt my feelings.)
4. Talk to a trusted friend or counselor about your unforgiveness. Holding it in can manifest itself in different ways. With past clients, I saw unforgiveness manifest itself through eating disorders, self-destructive behaviors, addictions of all forms, multiple marriages and divorces for one person, and an inability to have any close relationships.
5. Keep in mind that sometimes forgiveness transcends human understanding and the power to forgive comes from God. There are two ladies who have appeared on national television from our church telling their story of forgiveness. It is the story of a drunk driver and the sister whose brother the drunk driver killed. Months after the driver served her time in jail and court-ordered substance abuse treatment, the driver and sister saw each other at church. As the sister walked toward the driver, she was overcome with the feelings

and words to say "I forgive you because God forgives you." The sister did not know what she said until after she said it, but the driver collapsed in her arms, wept and thanked her for her forgiveness. They have built a strong friendship and now give talks around the nation to MADD and SADD groups to spread a message of hope and forgiveness.

6. If you say you won't forgive, then you must realize you are saying you have more power and authority than God over forgiveness. How can this be true? You are merely human.

7. Ask yourself if there is anything for which you need to forgive yourself. It has been amazing over the years to watch people torture themselves by not forgiving themselves for something they did. For example, I counseled a few college girls who had abortions during their high school years. They developed eating disorders as a way of 'punishing' themselves for what they did. I counseled a married woman in her early 30's who had aborted their first child. They had three children by the time we had met, yet she was having difficulty forgiving herself and seeing sexual intimacy as a positive in her marriage. What helped these women start forgiving themselves was acknowledging the hurt, pain, and loss of a baby. By naming their children and writing letters to them (one of them made a little spot in their backyard flower bed as a memorial), they were able to make a connection with a person rather than the act of the abortion. It made it human for them. They all realized that only God gave them enough power, strength, and wisdom to understand how to forgive themselves and

move on while preserving the memory of their loss.

8. Remember God can and does forgive. There is nothing you have done that God doesn't already know about. Ask yourself, "Am I hiding behind the guilt (I did something wrong) or shame (I am what's wrong)?" Do you believe there is something in your past that is unforgivable? If that were the case, then there is no need for the New Testament that talks about Jesus, or the church of today that started over 2,000 years ago. Just when you think you cannot be forgiven, think again.

CHAPTER 6

SPRING - A TIME OF
HOPE AND RENEWAL

A time to be born, a time to plant,
A time to heal, a time to build, a time to keep,
A time to mend. A time for peace.
        --Ecclesiastes, 3 various verses

As I am writing this chapter, spring has almost arrived here in Michigan. I say 'almost' because in the Midwest, we can get snow in April after a beautiful week of spring-like weather. I begin to trust it is truly spring when we have two solid weeks of warmer weather!

How about you? Are you ever reluctant to trust you are 'out of the woods' in a situation until consistency of the new order has taken place? If you are still defrosting from a particularly difficult winter season in life, you might find it difficult, at first, to enjoy and trust the new spring season.   You are in good company!

Indicators you are in a spring season:
1. You have a new, positive outlook about a previous winter season.
2. You have a more positive outlook on life in general.
3. You approach people and situations with a more proactive mindset.
4. You see loved ones with a fresh, new perspective.
5. You have more physical, emotional, and spiritual energy.
6. You have more self-confidence.
7. You think, "I can conquer anything!"

If you checked off one item, you are entering into a spring season. If you checked off three or more, you are already in your spring season.

Imagine for a moment, a spring setting.   The smell of fresh air, grass turning green, colorful flowers blooming, and the birds singing. I enjoy seeing color in our yard as our perennials have pushed up and bloomed. I am thankful that I get to see the renewal of color and lushness every new year.

FINALLY, SPRING!

My mother chose a very difficult life for herself. For 33 years, she spent her life in the darkest, coldest winter season and never approached a different season. She became an alcoholic within my first year of life, and that, coupled with her bipolar disorder, made life difficult for her and for us, her family. She made many bad choices, which cost her and us so much. Her suicide attempts; verbal, emotional and physical abuse; extreme mood swings; drunken states;

and severe depression kept her and us from enjoying any life at home.

In 1986, one month before I was to start college, my mother's fever-pitch manic state and belief she could quit drinking alcohol cold turkey landed her in the hospital. Throughout her three-week stay at rehab, the family was never involved in her recovery process. She was an angry drunk, and an angry recovering alcoholic. I was glad to be going off to college to get away from the chaos!

My mother managed to stay sober until her death, 15 years later. Although she didn't drink, she still behaved as an alcoholic. She acted and thought the same way and still placed blame on everyone and everything else, never taking responsibility. In the recovery field, the term that is used to describe this person is a 'dry drunk.'

In 1996, my mom had a heart attack. I got to the hospital when she was at her worst, and was either going to turn a corner, or die. When I first walked into her ICU room, all I saw were tubes and an oxygen mask. For the first time in my life, I saw her as a frail human being. It was at that moment of seeing her that a huge wave of relief came over me and I was able to finally believe and accept in my heart that I forgave her for all the past hurt and pain she caused. That was totally a God thing, and not me! My human attempts to forgive her failed miserably over the years. Now I was at peace knowing that if she died, I had forgiven her and would tell her that.

My mom lived through her close call of death, and I let her know she had a 'second chance' at life. I truly believed she appreciated that she lived through that experience, but it didn't seem to change her outlook on her own life or give her a desire to make positive changes.

It wasn't until 1997 that I told my mom I forgave her. We made a summer trip up to Chicago and stopped to see Mom. I let Jon know that I wanted to talk to her and needed time alone. He and my daughter went across the street to the park while I talked to her. I referred back to the time of her heart attack and what it was like seeing her hooked up to oxygen and machines and how God took away my burden of unforgiveness towards her. Her response?

She laughed and said "I heard you say this before."

"Yeah, mom, but this time is different. I have absolutely no anger towards you anymore. Before when I said I forgave you, I was still angry."

She stared at me for a moment and then said, "Yeah, well there has been a lot I have needed to forgive you about as well."

"Well, why don't you tell me, so I know?"

"No forget it. I don't want to talk about it."

"You always do this. You say something and then you try to avoid backing up your claim. You know, I just came here because I felt led to tell you this now that I forgive you. Whenever you're ready to accept it is fine. Just know that I love you no matter what."

My mom was silent and did not respond after that. She attempted to make small talk, but then said she needed to go and meet friends down in the lobby. I could tell by her body language and fumbling over words that I had made her uncomfortable. I had walked away feeling relieved that I told her what I needed to say for over a year.

From 1998 until her death in 2001, Mom steadily declined physically and emotionally. She was in and out of the mental hospital numerous times, and did not take her medication correctly. Her health was very poor, which made matters worse. She had a very grandiose manic state in summer, 2000, and then crashed into a severe depression from which she never recovered.

In May 2001, when I was in Chicago to tell my mom she was dying of cancer and to make funeral arrangements, I felt a greater purpose in being there for my mom. I was staying at a friend's house during this time, and I woke up very early on a Saturday morning to the feeling that I needed to share with my mom what has brought me joy through the hard times. I was to present it as the 'gift' that I received when I was 16 years old. When I went to see mom that morning at the hospital, we talked for a while about plans, but then I asked her if she'd like to hear about a gift I received that is also available to her. She let me share how important my faith in God had been to me. I had accepted the gift of Jesus to become personal and that Jesus made it possible to bridge the gap between me and God. This was the great news I wanted her to have the opportunity to hear and accept. She said she was interested in that gift because of what she had witnessed over the years with me and my husband, Jon. She witnessed how Jon and I handled conflict positively, showed unconditional love toward each other, how that love spilled over into raising our girls with respect and consistency, how we depended on God through tough times, and how we built a spiritual base for our family through Bible studies, church, and having the girls involved in church classes to learn more about God. She saw we were building a spiritual legacy that provided love, hope, and joy. It was an environment she never knew how to develop in her own marriage and family. So I lead her through a simple prayer where she accepted that she made many mistakes in her life and was ready to accept God. She understood for the first time that

Jesus sacrificing His life on the cross was the gift that God gave so that we could go to paradise in Heaven. It was hard for her, at first, to understand that it could be so simple. Her religion taught her that she had to do all the right things to get into heaven. Grace and mercy are really very simple, yet as humans, we make them so complex.

For the first time in my mother's life, she felt a tremendous burden being lifted, and had a few short weeks to enjoy her newfound freedom in a spring season. It was completely foreign to her, but she embraced it.

How about you? Have you felt that a 'cloud' has been lifted and is allowing you to see your life with a new perspective? Do you approach this new perspective with fear or do you embrace it?

EMBRACING YOUR NEW PERSPECTIVE

Consider asking yourself these questions to become more comfortable with your fresh, new perspective:

1   What new, fresh perspective have I learned about a person, or situation?
2   Is there anything holding me back? Please identify
3   If I'm holding back, how is it helping me?
4   What steps can I take to become more comfortable with this new perspective?
5   How will this new perspective help me move forward in life?

DISCOVERING YOUR SPRING

Sometimes, you can keep yourself from a spring season because you believe there is nothing you can do about a person or situation. This is often a reactive stance rather than being proactive. If you believe you have no options, you don't. When it comes to other people, whom you cannot control or change, convert your situation into a learning experience.

Often times you may ask for the person or situation to change, but for whatever reason, the person or situation does not change. This is the most difficult energy drainer to have. Although it may be hard to accept, sometimes your own changed attitude will help manage unchanged circumstances. If you are in a situation where your physical or emotional well being is threatened or if someone else is being threatened in anyway, then further intervention needs to be sought. If you are in a tough situation that is consuming a lot of emotional and/or physical energy, here are some steps to consider:

1. Start with the belief that you deserve better. If you don't, your goal will become a 'band aid' you can use to cover over the problem rather than resolving the issue so that it doesn't return. It becomes a quick fix rather than a lifestyle change. "Band aids" could look like addictions, running away from the person or situation, or placing all blame on the person or situation rather than taking responsibility for your part.

2. Solicit help and guidance from others. You temporarily might not have the strength to do things on your own.

3. Seek out law enforcement protection if necessary. Your life and the lives of your children (if applicable) need to be protected and saved.
4. Many turn to prayer in times of need. If that resonates with you, ask how your attitude can change even if the person doesn't.

Consider these questions to 'see' or develop spring moments in your life:

1. What person or situation has been draining me for a while?
2. What have I done in the past to make this better?
3. What is still keeping me in the 'winter' mentality rather than seeing the spring season?
4. What action(s) am I willing to take to see this differently?

HANNAH'S COMPLETE RECOVERY

The doctors were leery about sending Hannah home. She was barely eating and only making minimal progress with her occupational and physical therapy. She had one last potential complication toward the end of her hospital stay when her last chest tube was getting air in it and had to be removed. She had an x-ray for the next two days to ensure she didn't have fluid build-up in her lungs. After 21 days in the hospital, we were all finally able to go home.

Jon and I had decided even before she left the hospital that we would slowly wean her off her anti-seizure medication, Phenobarbital. Her follow-up EEG's showed no seizure activity and she only had seizures the day after her cardiac arrests. It was risky, but we noticed how much of the old Hannah was coming back the less Phenobarbital she received. We felt confident we were doing the right thing, despite what the neurology department was telling us.

The first week home was rough. Hannah was frustrated with herself because she wanted to do more physical activity, but just didn't have the strength yet. As each day went by, she would eat a little more, and gain back more of her fine and large motor skills. By her third week, she started walking again and was speaking more. We considered that complete recovery. Seeing her now, no one would ever know she fought so hard for her life. She is like any other strong-willed, fiery redhead! She is a walking miracle. All the doctors and nurses involved in her care believe that, too!

We had come out of such a difficult winter season, and after only three weeks home, we were able to enjoy our precious Hannah again. We knew we were out of the woods and celebrated the return of our family by spending a weekend at a fun hotel with an indoor water park. We had a new appreciation for life and for our family unit. I had nothing but gratefulness and praise for God who brought us through the most blinding snowstorm we had ever experienced. God's strength absolutely kept us going when we had none. We were grateful to have the opportunity to enjoy our spring.

WHO IS THIS?

When I first started dating Jon, I didn't know what to think. He was so different from all the other guys I had dated. He treated me with respect, love, and sincerity. He was the first guy whom I still really liked after our first month of dating. He told me he loved me after only dating for one month. That had never happened with other guys I had dated. I never allowed it. Because of my childhood, I didn't feel worthy of being loved or cared for. It was uncomfortable for me in our first few months together because my previous dating experiences left me hurt and confused. It was hard for me to believe that I could love someone who would return that love and love me unconditionally! For the first time in my life, someone loved me even when I wasn't very nice. Jon accepted me for who I was, warts and all. Because I was able to have a human experience with unconditional love, I started to see God as a loving being, too.

What has been your pattern for relationships? Can you give and receive unconditional love? Unconditional love doesn't have an 'if,' 'and', or 'but' attached to it.

Jon and I became engaged one year after we started dating. We were engaged for three and a half years because I didn't want to get married until I was a college graduate. So, three weeks after graduation, we were married. Our marriage has weathered through all of the seasons of life several times over. But I am forever grateful for how the seasons have fine-tuned our marriage and have allowed us to enjoy many spring and summer moments in our married life.

Have you ever encountered a person or situation that seemed so positively different that it was hard to believe it was real? Has that person or situation given you a refreshing outlook on yourself and your life that represents spring in your life? Use the steps below to evaluate your appreciation and glean more insight into your life. Remember, writing these steps out allows you to see the power and impact a season can have on your life perspective.

STEP 1: THE SITUATION

Describe a current or past spring season in your life. Who is with you? What are you doing? What is your perspective about the situation? The people involved? How do you see yourself? (Confident, happy, purposeful, etc). What is your view of God?

STEP 2: A SEASONAL SHIFT

What changed in your situation that ended your spring season? Was it something you could control? Was there some action or behavior on your part that ended your spring season? What is your view of God during this step?

STEP 3: LIFE APPLICATION

What did you learn about yourself and/or God with this event or moment?

"Hope springs eternal" is a common phrase you might have heard along the way in your life. Hope brings renewal, healing, and energy. I hope you are now energized to keep moving forward in your quest for a happier, healthier, more fulfilling life!

PART III

Now What?

CHAPTER 7

EVALUATING "IF"

Going through your different seasons of life, you might want to know what to do with the conclusions you reached in each season's evaluation. We will be taking a look at "What if God were to be included in your life?" What would it mean?

Before jumping into that, you must evaluate if you are even open to a paradigm shift, or shift in mindset. Are you willing to look outside your comfort zone?

EXERCISE:

Connect the set of nine dots, with 4 straight lines, without lifting your pen or pencil.

• • •

• • •

• • •

• • •

• • •

• • •

• • •

• • •

• • •

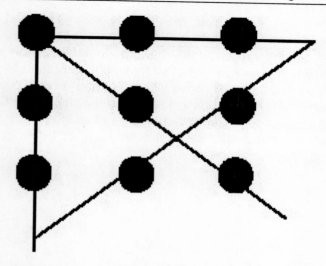

What do you notice about how the dots are connected? You had to draw outside the box. Likewise in evaluating if God could be a part of your life, you need to be willing to look outside your box and move out of your comfort zone to see the possibilities.

Misery is an option. I like using the analogy of a frog in boiling water. If you put a frog in boiling water, it will jump right out. If you put a frog in warm water and slowly turn up the heat to boil, it dies. Why? It learned to tolerate the heat and didn't know when it was too hot. Same is true for our lives. It amazes me how many people are unaware of how miserable they really are, but their words and actions show it loud and clear. They choose to be negative, critical, cynical and stressed out. They often have no life balance and complain rather than be proactive to change anything.

It is also amazing how when people are aware of their misery, they'll stick with it because it's comfortable. I would like to suggest learning to become comfortable with the uncomfortable and see what great life could be waiting for you!

Like drawing outside the box, looking outside your box will mean you must see yourself as human to see God. You might be highly intelligent and very successful and believe you don't need anything, including God! Ask yourself "Is all my success and intellect bringing all the happiness and contentment that I ever could possibly want and need?"

CHAPTER 8

YOUR LIFE'S ROAD MAP

God has made everything beautiful in its time. Men cannot fathom what has been done from beginning to end. . . .Whatever is has already been, and what will be has been before.

--Ecclesiastes 3:11, 15

Several years ago when I went through my CPE experience, I had a choice to make about the life path I was choosing. I could remain on my current path or change course. Relying on me as a compass for life direction proved to be futile. I was miserable. I felt like a hamster on a spinning wheel with no way of getting off or getting anywhere!

As I have worked with people over the years, I have noticed that when it comes to accepting God into their lives, they often believe that they would have to 'give up' their lives. Knowing God isn't like a diet – a way to deprive you of good tasting food. If you could 'think outside your box' for a moment, you might see that including God isn't about what you're giving up. Rather, it is about what you are getting. The only thing you are giving up is control over your life. My winter seasons have taught me a very tough lesson over the years; control is an illusion. I guess you'd be giving up the illusion of control.

CHARTING YOUR COURSE

Here is an exercise you could do that could help you logically map out your life with and without God.

1. Fold a sheet vertically in half. Or if you are doing this on computer, make a four-box table.
2. One column reads "Life benefits without God" and the other reads "Life benefits with God."
3. Flip the page and make two different columns reading "Life without God will lead to..." and "Life with God will lead to...."
4. Take your time filling this out. Continue to add to your columns until you believe it is complete. Try not to take more than a week to do this. Be honest and truthful with yourself.

Below is a beginning example of my step process to evaluate God after my CPE experience:

Life benefits without God	Life benefits with God
No rules, own freedom	Less stress
No guilt	Clearer direction
	No confusion
	Peace
	Strength
	Less worry
	No fear
	Hope
Life without God will lead to...	Life with God will lead to...
More fear	Greater fulfillment
More chaos	Happiness
Less direction, jumping around	A life better than ever imagined
No hope	Freedom from my own demands
Divorce	Contentment
Less confidence	
More negative consequences of my actions	
Loneliness	

As you can see, for me, putting God back in my life outweighed leaving Him out. Maybe you have never had any type of experience with religion or God and have no idea what a life with God would look like. For everything you put in your left column, write down the opposite of it in the right column. Remember to think outside your box (your current reality). By looking at your table, you may realize some truths of which you were unaware. If you still are having difficulty filling it out, seek out a spiritual and non-spiritual friend to help.

You do have the control and power to choose your own course.

CHAPTER 9

THE LIFE YOU HAVE ALWAYS WANTED

For we are God's workmanship, created in Christ Jesus to do good works, which God prepared in advance for us to do.

--Ephesians 2:10

Notice the words *in advance*, meaning that even before you were born, God had a purpose for your life. You might still be feeling directionless, but again, you have a choice as to whether you will allow God to be a compass for you. This verse has had more impact on me in recent years because of a few words my mom told me right before she died.

AN INITIAL SHOCK

Two weeks before my mother's death, I had a strong prompting that I needed to go see my mom one more time before she died. I felt I needed to go to provide comfort, support, and to help her 'let go.' I wasn't expecting to really talk or converse with her because by then, she was on large doses of morphine for pain and was in a lucid state. Two days later, I was in Chicago to pray for her, read to her, and whatever else was needed. I considered my mother's pending death to be a brief autumn season because of the changes that would occur. I never imagined it would bring a life-altering perspective.

When I arrived at the nursing home, the hospice nurse had just finished her visit, so my mom was awake and somewhat alert. I got an update from the nurse on her deteriorating condition, and then went in her room.

When I walked in, my mom made immediate eye contact with me and said, "Lynn, I tried to abort you."

She started crying and was apologizing, but I went over to her bedside, stroked her head and said, "It's okay, mom, I forgive you. It's okay. I already know."

She stopped crying immediately, looked me straight in the eyes and said, "How do you know?"

"Because God revealed it to me two weeks ago. He prepared me for this moment." She stared at me with complete bewilderment, wondering how something she kept a secret for 33 years could possibly have already been known.

What she didn't know was that two weeks prior to her confession, when I was at home praying to God and asking why my mom was still fighting to live, I asked if there was something she needed to release before dying. God truly did speak to me to prepare me for my mother's confession. When I asked God if there was something that was holding back mom, He very clearly said, "She tried to abort you." At that time, I didn't think much of those words. It took me back to the times when my mom had told me I was a mistake, and I was her cross to bear. In my mind, I had already believed it because of those words she had said to me over the years. I was in shock that God had said to me earlier the exact words my mother used.

When my mom drifted off into her semi-conscious state, the impact of what occurred just hit me. Had God not prepared me a few weeks prior to my mom's confession, I would have had a devastating time working through that. I did walk out of my mom's room for the rest of that day to deal with the emotions that were surfacing. The hurt, anger, sadness and confusion were all there. What was going on in Mom's life at that time that she wanted to get rid of me? Throughout this time, I could feel God's hand just guiding me to see my mom through His eyes and not to get caught up in the confession. I was still in awe and so grateful that God truly prepared me for such a blow ahead of time.

As I drove home the next day, I realized that I was able to do what I was prompted to do: I let her 'let go.' She had carried the burden of the attempted abortion for all those years, buried it for so many years, which tore our family apart. Now she was free. My brother said that when he visited her the next day, she kept saying "Thank you." She never regained consciousness like she had when I last saw her. She passed away 12 days later.

I was amazed at how much more I loved my mom and was able to see her as a human being. I don't know what her state of mind was when she was pregnant with me. I was overcome with thoughts of gratefulness: grateful that I was born; grateful that she didn't treat me any worse than the rest of my siblings; grateful that she tried to make up for it with fleeting moments of play and reading to me; and grateful that in her moments of not being drunk, she attempted to really connect with me.

Can you see how the Ephesians 2:10 passage applies here? Even when I was in my mother's womb as she attempted to abort me, God had a greater plan even before I was born. He protected me so that I would be born to live out the purpose He has for my life. It is amazing how from beginning to end, if you are willing, God can play a significant part in your life!

In the days after burying my mom, the only way I could seek out assurance that I was special and loved and that I really had a reason to be on this earth, was to turn to scripture. People and circumstances over the years never could fully answer the questions in my mind as to why I was here. The following scripture were words I had read many times before, but with my new knowledge, these words brought me comfort in knowing that where humans fail, God prevails.

"For you created my inmost being; you knit me together in my mother's womb. I praise you because I am fearfully and wonderfully made; your works are wonderful, I know that full well. My frame was not hidden from you when I was made in the secret place. When I was woven together in the depths of the earth, your eyes saw my unformed body. All the days ordained for me were written in your book before one of them came to be."

Psalm 139:13-16

Can you relate to thoughts and feelings of worthlessness, directionless, hopelessness and being unloved?

As you begin to understand what your purpose is here on earth, I'd like you to look over the past chapters and how you worked through the steps in each season of life. Do you notice any common themes or patterns? What have those steps revealed about you? God? Those commonalities play into your life purpose.

MANY PEOPLE WITH DIFFERENT BACKGROUNDS, SAME THEME

Over the years, I have had the privilege of working with a variety of people from those with wounded upbringings to very successful people who were driven to have more. The overwhelming themes (needs, really) from this entire spectrum of people has been this: They seek acceptance, unconditional love, and a sense of belonging, and use whatever means to fill those voids. Those means can include staying busy, working too much, seeking identity through their children, losing themselves in addictions, etc. Whatever allows you to turn off your emotions, focus completely on others or completely on the self, or allows you to function from an intellectual approach to life, could explain why you have been so turned off by God. Having a relationship with God goes beyond pure intellect; it involves the heart.

In America, we are a task-driven, performance-oriented society. We truly believe we can do and have it all. If we don't, we can just work harder and it will all work out. No wonder depression is so rampant in society! We are stressed out hoping to find happiness and fulfillment, yet when we think we have 'arrived,' it's not enough, or it's not good enough, so we want more. Do you see the vicious cycle that is created?

I conducted a workshop for an organization entitled "Ignite Your Passion." I started out my talk by giving an example of a client who came to me stressed out, burned out, ready to quit a job, and exhausted. She just wanted to check out from life for a while. Can you relate? Well, many in the audience did, and they spent the next two and a half hours exploring and working through how they can ignite or reignite their passion for life. What would your life look like if you had energy, passion and direction? Below are some tips of how to regain energy and passion.

Tips to (re)ignite your passion:

1. *Simplify.* What have I made more complicated in my life that can really be simplified? A while back, we received a little booklet from Starbucks to educate the public on how to order at one of their stores. It was amazing all the different ways you could order, and at the end of the booklet, they gave an example statement of what to say. My husband and I just laughed because who would have thought ordering coffee would become so complicated!

2. *Let Go.* Am I hanging on to people or situations that I really cannot control? Am I so performance driven that I'm forgetting how to be 'in the moment?'

3. *Define Boundaries.* Is "no" in my vocabulary? Am I allowing people or situations to take advantage of me? Am I taking people or situations for granted?

4. *Balance.* Am I stressed out or burned out? Am I easily frustrated? Is my mind doing one thing, but focused on something else? Am I overwhelmed with the demands of work and/ or home?

5. *Ask yourself, "What's important?"* If you were to 'dummy down' your complex, multi-faceted life, would you say you are living what is truly most important to you? Passion stems from living who you are!

PIVOTING YOUR LIFE CIRCUMSTANCES

The movie "A Beautiful Life" told the story of an Italian Jewish father and son who were in Nazi concentration camps. As the war raged on, the father protected his son from the atrocities by describing what was being told or witnessed with a positive spin. No matter what 'war' may be raging inside of you, try to pivot and find some good in your past or current circumstances.

In 1997, I had a client who came to me because she was overwhelmed with the stress and anger over a situation involving the two most important people in her life. One was about to go to jail, and the other was responsible for putting him there. The trial was purely based on circumstantial evidence and this client was amazed that her loved one was convicted and had to serve time. She was totally turned off to God and the church they had attended because of the judgmental attitudes they portrayed about her situation. She was frustrated and needed a non-judgmental outlet to vent. When she first came to me, she interviewed me for 15 minutes because she was at a critical point in her circumstances and felt she couldn't trust anyone.

I guess I said the right things, because that day we started our work together that lasted over one year.

As the weeks and events unfolded in her situation, our time together focused on how she was processing her feelings and working through the war that was raging inside her. She had been brought up in the church and understood the basics, but those basics were blown out of the water when this tremendous 'storm' hit her life.

I remember when she started turning a corner in her view towards God. I asked her, "It seems that God has shut many doors for you. Are you now seeing an open window, even just a crack?" She answered that question two-fold. One, where she saw absolutely no hope in her situation, she was now seeing a glimmer that the situation would not turn out as bad as it could have been. Two, where her heart and mind were totally closed to God, there was now an opportunity to be open to exploring if she wanted God back in her life.

When the situation played itself out and the consequences were set, there was a lot of grief, sadness, and letting go this client had to do. As she moved through that process, she gradually found her own baby steps back to God. It was an exhausting process, but one that she was thankful for. Her 'storm' knocked her down for some time, but it didn't wipe her out.

Just before my family and I moved out of state, I received a thank you and update note from this client. Tears of joy ran down my face as I read her letter telling me of all the good that came from that bad situation, and how being involved in a new church and new people had renewed her faith in God and in people. It was made possible because she made the conscious choice to pivot and see a different perspective on her life.

How about you? Are you willing to pivot out of your current life to see what's on the other side? A new horizon? A new perspective? Is there a 'new' life waiting for you?

YOUR 'NEW' LIFE

Can you picture your passionate, happy life? With individuals and audiences, I have had them draw a picture of their passionate, focused life they see themselves living six months from that day of drawing the picture. When you are able to at least envision it, there is room to actually achieve it. Some have discovered that what they believed brought them or will bring happiness is only temporary. They cannot guarantee it will always bring them contentment.

There is only one 'sure' thing that can bring the contentment, peace, hope, and direction that, perhaps, you have never experienced or have not experienced in a very long time. That is a personal relationship with God. It has nothing to do with religion. Religion is made up of the rules and assumptions you must follow that allow you access to God. A relationship is strictly between you and God – no middle person!

A BRIGHT SPOT AMIDST THE CHAOS

When I was 16, I started attending a Christian youth group because of one main reason: I had a huge crush on a guy. There was something different about him that intrigued me. Have you ever met someone like that?

I went weekly to the youth group because one, it was an escape from my alcoholic mom, and two, for the first time in my life, I was having fun. The group would do neat games and activities, and then the youth pastor would talk about God. It was different than attending church because we didn't recite learned prayers or sing and kneel at appropriate times. It was the first time I ever heard about having a personal relationship with God. I had no idea what that meant, but figured I'd keep investigating until something would hit me. I was searching and didn't even know it.

I attended the group's winter retreat where we had tons of fun and great speakers. One speaker in particular was talking about how God gave the gift of His son Jesus to show us what a relationship with God would be like. He used a verse out of Revelation that said "I stand at the door of your heart and knock. If anyone hears my voice and opens the door, I will come in." At that moment, my searching had turned into a need – the need to have someone, something beyond myself and my own strength to get me through the hell of living with an alcoholic parent. I needed help, peace and wisdom to keep me alive. I needed hope that my future could be better. I needed someone else's strength because the weight of the painful personal life I was trying to hide was too much to bear. I was so tired of life and only 16 years old! I asked Jesus into my heart that day. I still didn't fully understand what it meant or how and if my life would change, but for the first time, I had a hope and belief that I could actually have a life outside my dysfunctional home.

WHAT DOES A PERSONAL RELATIONSHIP MEAN?

Jesus said, *"I am the way and the truth and the life. No one comes to the Father except through me. If you really knew me, you would know my Father as well. From now on, you do know him and have seen him."*

John 14:6

Now I realize that you might be offended by the word "him." I can understand that. The perpetrators of my abuse were male. My father, who was not one of my abusers, was and is absent from my life. My original perception of God was that He was distant and absent. I could not make an emotional connection with God. Please note in the context of the Old and New Testament, the original Hebrew and Greek assigned the male gender words to God. God is supernatural, so He possesses both gender characteristics.

It took a while for me to warm up to the idea of trusting in something other than myself because of my childhood perceptions of God. When I finally asked Jesus into my heart, I acknowledged the fact that I had really made a mess of my life and was so confused, I couldn't continue messing up the way I was! No matter how smart and independent I believed I was (of course, I was 16!); I was saying I couldn't and didn't want to do it anymore.

I came from a religious upbringing where God was not 'personal.' If I wanted to do well in God's eyes, I had to pray to the saints, go to confession, and attend service at least weekly. The only way I learned about anything in the Bible was through the interpretation from the priest.

When I learned that God is not about religion's rules and regulations, but an actual relationship, I met the challenge to discover how I could actually communicate and pray only to God. The John 14:6 passage says that the way I could do that was to accept Jesus and the sacrifice He made on the cross on my behalf. Accepting His work on the cross meant that I accepted Jesus as my savior; it meant that I believed He saved me from my sins and eternal darkness once I left this earth. Saying I accepted Jesus as my Lord meant I was willing to give the reins of my messed up life and let Him take over.

"Come to me, all you who are weary and burdened, and I will give you rest."
                                                              Matthew 11:28

I desperately needed rest. The burden and struggle of living with an alcoholic mother was too much. I needed someone, something else to relieve the pressure. I had to admit I no longer could do it on my own. For the stubborn, prideful, fiercely independent girl I was, that was not easy! But as soon as I prayed to have Jesus as my Lord and Savior, it was as if the weight of the world had been lifted. As I started a new journey in relationship with God, a whole new life was opened up for me.

How about you? Are you ready and willing to say, "Okay, I can't do life on my own anymore?" God meets us all individually. Your experience with God is always your own, but can serve as an inspiration to others. It is always nice to meet with people who have been where you are.

Below is a suggested prayer you can pray that will allow you to take action in moving forward to that more fulfilling, focused life that *GOD HAS DESIGNED*

FOR YOU! Feel free to say the words out loud if you are ready.

> *God, I acknowledge that I have made mistakes and have sinned against you. Please forgive me. I realize that 'sin' is everything that has kept me from a relationship with you. I now accept Jesus as my Lord and Savior to bring me into a personal relationship with you and believe that you have always loved me despite my doing the things that have hurt you and me. Thank you for the gift of Jesus that allows me to stand before you now as a child of God. Amen.*

OKAY, NOW WHAT?

First of all, if you prayed the above prayer, congratulations! You are a new creation, a new life to be lived!

This book is not the end of your journey; it is only the beginning. How do you begin your journey? Here are a few suggestions to get you started moving forward. You're a new student of life. There is so much waiting for you to learn!

1. Purchase a Bible to help you learn about who God really is. The New International, New American Standard or Living Bible would be very useful for you. The study Bibles are especially helpful in explaining difficult passages or verses. Feel free to start with the gospels in the New Testament –(Matthew, Mark, Luke and John) to learn more about the ministry of Jesus. The Bible has so much to teach you about who God really is, what His characteristics are, and how the stories of the people of Biblical times apply to your own life

now. Think of the Bible as your fuel and energy to learn about living a passionate, purposeful life!

2.   You can't start a new life on your own. Are there people in your current life that you respect because of their faith? If so, ask to attend their church or for help finding a church. What is important for you in a church? Do you want to seek out a church that is focused on the Bible and a personal relationship with God rather than rules and regulations? You want to be in a church that 'fits' for you. What fits for some might not fit for others. Visit different churches to get a feel for what you are looking for. You want a church that has enough to offer to help you learn and grow, with opportunities to give back to others when you are ready.

3.   There are non-denominational Bible studies in every community. If there is a large church in your community or one nearby, you can inquire as to what's available. Surf the web. The larger churches that offer many different ministries within one church will be found on the Internet. There is also an inter-faith, international Bible study called Bible Study Fellowship. The way you build relationships with others is to spend time and get to know them. Bible study allows you to spend time in God's word to learn more about Him.

I'M NOT READY TO MOVE AHEAD

Congratulations! You read through this book, so that says something about perseverance in your character. You have decided that the prayer on the previous page is just not for you.....yet. That is okay! God prompts you at the perfect time. You will know when you are ready. If the previous chapters have provoked thoughts you never realized you had, find a trusted friend or family member to talk through it. I have found spiritual mentors (people I respect further along in the faith) within different churches to help me sort through my most challenging times. If it requires further investigation and you're willing to be a little uncomfortable, seek out a clergyperson to help answer questions. Ask friends or family to refer you to someone if you don't want to seek clergy on your own. If you continue looking, you will find the answers. That is God's promise to you.

CHAPTER 10

YOUR TRUE CORE

Recently relocated, my client had planned to climb the corporate ladder of his new company the way he did at his other places of employment. He was intelligent with a wealth of expertise that made him good at just about anything he did. Success came easy for him, and at a young age, he accomplished more than some people do in their entire career.

After attending one of my workshops entitled "Live Out Loud!" this man saw that he was missing a significant part of his life. At first, he was unable to recognize the missing part.

As he continued his coaching, he discovered that he had ignored his spiritual side in pursuit of career success. All his success could not mask the void he had experienced for so many years. No matter how much success he had, it was never good enough. He always wanted something more. His craving for more left him empty in the past, but now he realized that allowing God in his life would bring him more fulfillment because there was nothing else to turn to. Exploring God was his last hope for happiness. Once he discovered how to tap into a resource other than himself, total transformation occurred in his life. He learned what his true life purpose was and how his career was only an extension of that purpose. His original definition of success was to climb the corporate ladder. After coaching, he changed his idea of success to include "living with personal, professional and spiritual integrity." He was able to discover what his true core (purpose) was.

INDIANA JONES AND THE LAST CRUSADE

For those who might not have seen this movie, it is about the search by Indiana Jones, an archeologist, and his father for the Holy Grail. The search takes them to caverns, and the only way to navigate through them is to use the dad's notes for a safe passage. Indiana's father is injured so Indiana himself must get to the Holy Grail. He comes to a point in the journey where he stands at the edge of a huge abyss. He sees the other side and the continuation of the path to the grail, but he has no idea how to get across. After viewing the notes, Indiana realizes the only way he can get across is to 'take a step of faith' and believe that he will be able to miraculously walk across air. After a deep breath, he steps out and indeed is able to walk. It is then that the pathway across the abyss is revealed. When you are able to take a courageous step into something you're not sure of, you open a whole new world.

How about you? Does taking a 'step of faith' across the abyss seem too daring for you? Are you willing to open yourself up to see the other side as a whole new world that includes God? You'll never know what you are missing unless you take that step. The client in the previous section did, and now lives a focused life with passion, purpose and a true love for God.

HOW DO I DISCOVER MY TRUE CORE?

In order to live a focused, purposeful life, your journey will consist of the steps below to formulate a life purpose statement. Let us look at the differences between a purpose statement and a personal mission statement.

PERSONAL MISSION STATEMENT	PURPOSE STATEMENT
Focus is set on goal(s) to achieve.	Focus is on living out lifelong goals daily.
Short-term, often during particular time of life (i.e. while unemployed, strategically network with others in desired fields of interest)	Long-term(lifelong). Living out whom you are no matter what role(s) or time of life you are in.
Fluctuates, according to the changing needs of person.	Unchanging. A person's role or function might change over time, but the purpose for that person's life is seen through common themes of those different roles.

STEP 1: YOUR CORE VALUES

Values are part of the foundation for your life purpose. You live out your values on a daily basis.

Personal Core Values

Exercise:

Step 1: From the list of core values, check the top 20 values most important to you.

Step 2. From the list of core values checked, circle the 10 most important values.

Step 3: Pick the top three that have been MOST consistent over the years.

Suggestion:

Pick the values that have been most consistent for you throughout the years. Do not pick ones you wish to have.

The three personal values most important to me are...

_____   _____   _____

Achievement	Aesthetics	Affiliation
Artistic Creativity	Autonomy/ Independence	Advancement and Promotion
Adventure	Affection (love and caring)	Arts
Change and Variety	Character	Chaos
Community Activity	Commute	Competition
Creativity	Challenging problems	Charity
Close relationships	Community	Compassion
Competence	Competition	Cooperation
Country	Creativity	Dual-Careers
Excitement	Fast Pace	Global Focus
Impact Society	Influence People	Intellectual Status
Knowledge	Legacy	Lifestyle Integration
Location	Loyalty	Make Decisions

Minimize Stress

Moral Fulfillment

Power and Authority

Profit, Gain

Recognition

Self-realization

Time Freedom

Work under Pressure

Ecological awareness

Efficiency

Excellence

Faith

Fast-paced work

Freedom

Having a family

Honesty

Inner harmony

Involvement

Leadership

Market position

Money

Uniqueness

Power and authority

Purity

Religion

Security

Service to others

Stability

Time freedom

Wealth

Mobility

Multi-Cultural Affiliation

Precision Work

Public Contact

Risk

Stability

Travel

Work With Others

Economic security

Ethical practice

Excitement

Fame

Fidelity

Friendships

Helping other people

Independence

Integrity

Job tranquility

Location

Meaningful work

Nature

Physical challenge

Privacy

Quality relationships

Reputation

Self-respect

Sophistication

Status

Trust

Moral Affiliation

Physical Challenge

Prestige

Pure Challenge

Security

Supervision

Work Alone

Democracy

Effectiveness

Health

Expertise

Fast living

Financial gain

Growth

Helping society

Influencing Others

Intellectual status

Knowledge

Loyalty

Merit

Wisdom

Pleasure

Public service

Respect from others

Accountability

Serenity

Spirituality

Supervising others

Truth

STEP 2: PAST/CURRENT EXPERIENCES

Explore five to ten experiences in the past five years when you felt you were living and being "on purpose." If you must go back further than five years, that's fine. Your purpose statement is unique to you. In fact, you have been living out your purpose in some way, even if you are not conscious of it. That means you can plumb your past to find your purpose. For each of the experiences you list, write a paragraph about each of these experiences. Write down what you did, where you were, what the outcome was, how you felt. And, the paragraph should answer the questions:

1. What was essential to my sense of being on purpose?
2. What about this experience was richly satisfying?
3. What was of value here for me?

Once you've written your paragraphs, underline the key words from each experience. Put all of the underlined words on a separate page. Examine them and find the commonalities, the themes among them. These are the phrases you will use to build your statement of purpose. In your experiences, can you identify if you were a leader, partner or follower?

STEP 3: HOW YOU ARE WIRED -- ARE YOU LIVING WHO YOU ARE?

Ask yourself the following questions:

1. How am I best motivated? Do I create and act on own ideas or am I a team player?
2. How do I best communicate? Do I need time to think or time to talk?
3. How do I work best? Am I a multi-tasker/need variety or am I uni-focused and like sequence?

4   How do I like to give and receive information? Do I need information in bullet points or do I need proof with lots of information?

STEP 4: YOUR GIFTS AND TALENTS

Put a check by the top three phrases that describe you:

1   Prefer hands-on experiments, concrete problems to solve
2   Curious, rational, intellectual, introspective. Prefer to design own work
3   Original, free-spirited, creative, artistic, musical
4   Helpful, cooperative, understanding, people-oriented
5   Persuasive, self-confident, extroverted, and risk-taker
6   Practical, methodical, efficient, orderly

Your purpose summary sheet:

Step1: My top three core values are
  A.
  B.
  C.

Step 2: Write down the key words from your paragraphs.

Step 3: My gifts and talents are
  a. Best motivated:
  b. Best communicate:
  c. Work best:
  d. Best to receive/give information:

Step 4: My top three phrases that describe me:
1.
2.
3.

In looking at your summary sheet, do you see any consistencies? What do you notice about yourself and what you contribute to others?

Your purpose is the very essence of who you are. It is what you are at the core and then how you live out your core to the world. This is where you can see how God has designed you to be in this world.

Looking over your summary sheet, plug in the above steps and see if the flow resonates to really describe who you are in any given environment. Your purpose statement is about you and how you function in this world.

My life purpose is to…..
Live out my core values of *STEP 1* by *STEP 2.* I am best motivated to live a passionate, purposeful life by creating an environment that is *STEP 3.* When all of the above steps are utilized, I am then able to live my gifts of *STEP 4.*

Below is an example of how to compile the life purpose statement.

My life purpose is to...
Live out my core values in which faith lays a foundation where integrity, transformation and discovery occur and bring challenge, focus and direction for myself and others. I am a mouthpiece for how to build relationships with God and others.

When I am in an environment that allows me to create and act on my own ideas, allows me to be part of a team, and provides variety and fast-pace, I am then able to live my qualities of being self-confident, free-spirited, creative, helpful, extroverted, and a risk-taker.

Crafting your life purpose statement might require more than just a quick run through this exercise. Take your time and think it over as you change words or phrases. When you feel you have reached completion of your statement, ask yourself:

1. Does this statement really resonate with me?
2. Does it describe me and who I have been over the years and how I envision myself impacting others in the future?
3. If I were to assign a percentage of how true this statement is to me right now, what would it be? Keep in mind that if it isn't 100 percent, that's okay. Mull over the statement for the next few weeks and evaluate daily or weekly how your life experiences for that week fit your purpose statement.

THE WATER BEARER AND HIS POTS

A water bearer in India had two large pots, each hung on each end of a pole, which he carried across his neck. One of the pots had a crack in it, and while the other pot was perfect and always delivered a full portion of water at the end of the long walk from the stream to the master's house. The cracked pot arrived only half full.

For a full two years this went on daily, with the bearer delivering only one and a half pots full of water in his master's house. Of course, the perfect pot was proud of its accomplishments. But the poor cracked pot was ashamed of its own imperfection, and miserable that it was able to accomplish only half of what it had been made to do. After two years of what it perceived to be a bitter failure, it spoke to the water bearer one day by the stream.

"I am ashamed of myself, and I want to apologize to you."

"Why?" asked the bearer. "What are you ashamed of?"

"I have been able, for these past two years, to deliver only half my load because this crack in my side causes water to leak out all the way back to your master's house. Because of my flaws, you have to do all of this work, and you don't get full value from your efforts," the pot said.

The water bearer felt sorry for the old cracked pot, and in his compassion he said, "As we return to the master's house, I want you to notice the beautiful flowers along the path."

Indeed, as they went up the hill, the old cracked pot took notice of the sun warming the beautiful wild flowers on the side of the path, and this cheered it some. But at the end of the trail, it still felt bad because it had leaked out half its load, and so again the pot apologized to the bearer for its failure.

The bearer said to the pot, "Did you notice that there were flowers only on your side of your path, but not on the other pot's side? That's because I have always known about your flaw, and I took advantage of it. I planted flower seeds on your side of the path, and every day while we walk back from the stream, you've watered them. For two years I have been able to pick these beautiful flowers to decorate my master's table. Without you being just the way you are, he would not have this beauty to grace his house."

Each of us has our own unique flaws. We're all cracked pots. But if we will allow it, our flaws will be used to grace His Father's table. In God's great economy, nothing goes to waste. Don't be afraid of your flaws. Acknowledge them, and you too can be the cause of beauty.

Know that in our weakness we find our strength.

Author Unknown

This story is an assurance that even though we are all 'cracked pots,' God still has a purpose for all of us! God desires a relationship with you so that you can see all the beauty He has intended for you to see and live. Are you ready, willing, and able to start a new life that includes a partnership with God? God is ready if you are.

About the Author

Lynn Jarrett, M.A., LCPC, is a life and business coach who has been helping people generate, accelerate, and perpetuate their personal and professional goals for over 15 years. Her current work as a coach and former work as a therapist has shown that many people form all walks of life desire to see how and if God fits into their lives.

Lynn lives in Michigan with her husband and three daughters. She can be contacted at Lynn@whybotherlooking.com

Printed in the United States
39206LVS00001B/242

9 781420 854510